"Concise ideas, clearly explained, plus a liberal touch of lighthearted-
ness, will make this a treasured addition to anyone's bookshelf."

—**Kitty Morse**, author of *The California
Farm Cookbook* and *365 Ways to
Cook Vegetarian*

"Like pirates, writers tend to bury their 'gold' —but under piles of
paper. Here's a system to shore up your writing bulwarks. The authors
map out a treasure chest of ideas. Captain Kidd would have loved it!"

—**Craig Arnold**, historian, San Diego
Maritime Museum, and author of *Eut-
erpe* and *Medea: The Classic Steam
Yacht*

"Writers accumulate paper. Oh, do they accumulate paper! Fortu-
nately, this book has ... good suggestions for managing all that
paper, and I happily recommend it when I teach my speechwriting
workshops."

—**Joan Detz**, author of *How to Write
and Give a Speech* and *Can You Say
a Few Words?*

"I flipped open *File ... Don't Pile!® for People Who Write* and immediately got an idea that I could use—and did. Then I found the entire
book filled with similar useful tips and techniques. It's great for any
writer, and for anyone for that matter."

—**Bert Decker**, author of *You've Got to
Be Believed to Be Heard*

"Whether you keep your writing records in files or on a computer,
this comprehensive, up-to-date manual should be an invaluable aid
in improving your systems and helping you become a more efficient
writer."

—**James Cross Giblin**, children's book
writer and editor, and author of *Writing Books for Young People*

# File . . . Don't Pile!®
## FOR PEOPLE WHO WRITE

ALSO BY PAT DORFF

File ... Don't Pile!®

# File . . . Don't Pile!®
## FOR PEOPLE WHO WRITE

Handling the Paper Flow
in the Workplace or Home Office

*by* PAT DORFF, EDITH FINE,
*and* JUDITH JOSEPHSON

ST. MARTIN'S PRESS
NEW YORK

Permission to reprint excerpts is gratefully acknowledged: Dieter Hildebrandt from *Pianoforte: A Social History of the Piano* © 1985 Dieter Hildebrandt, translated by Harriet Goodman © 1988 reprinted with the permission of George Braziller Inc. Caption from "Shoe" cartoon strip by Jeff MacNelly © 1988 Tribune Media Services, Inc. Quote from Audrey and Don Wood reprinted by the permission of Audrey and Don Wood. Alex Haley as quoted in *Northwest Airlines WorldTraveler* © 1992 reprinted with the permission of Skies America. Quote from Pam Conrad reprinted with the permission of Pam Conrad. Sandra Hirsh and Jean Kummerow from *LifeTypes* © 1989 Warner Books Inc., reprinted with the permission of Warner Books Inc. MBTI® quote on page 214 and MBTI® chart on pages 218–219 modified and reproduced by special permission of the publisher, Consulting Psychologists Press, Inc., Palo Alto, CA 94303 from the *Report Form for the Myers-Briggs Type Indicator*® by Isabel Briggs Myers, © 1987 by Peter B. Myers and Katharine D. Myers, all rights reserved; further reproduction is prohibited without the publisher's written consent. Susan Scanlon from the Winter 1985 issue of "The Type Reporter," © 1985 by Susan Scanlon reprinted with her permission.

Library of Congress Cataloging-in-Publication Data
Dorff, Pat.
    File—don't pile! : for people who write / Pat Dorff, Edith
Fine, and Judith Josephson.
        p.   cm.
    ISBN 0-312-10286-0
    1. Filing systems.   2. Paperwork (Office practice)—Management.
I. Fine, Edith Hope.   II. Josephson, Judith Pinkerton.   III. Title.
HF5736.D673   1994
651.5'3—dc20                                          93-42682
                                                          CIP

First Edition: May 1994

10   9   8   7   6   5   4   3   2   1

*To my parents, Victor Morack and Florence Lehman Morack,*
*who taught me to persevere.*

—PAT DORFF

*To our families, for their love, support, and encouragement.*

—EDITH FINE *and* JUDITH JOSEPHSON

# CONTENTS

Acknowledgments xi

Introduction xiii

**CHAPTER 1** **Facing the Mess** 1

My Side of the Mountain

Learning the Secret to Paper Control 4

**CHAPTER 2** **Digging In** 7

The Charge of the Light Brigade

Tackling the Paper Mess: The Five-Step

  Organization Plan 11

Persevering with Your Plan 28

**CHAPTER 3** **Setting Up a Filing System** 31

A Light in the Attic

Using the A–Z Method 34

Using the Prefix Method 38

Deciding Which Method to Use 43

Why Use a Pencil? 44

Color-Coding 44

**CHAPTER 4** **Cross-Referencing Files** 47

The Road Not Taken

Using SEE Cross-References 50

Using SEE ALSO Cross-References 55

Cross-Referencing from One Category to Another 57

Using REMINDER Cross-References 58

**CHAPTER 5** **Managing Pending Papers** 61

Some Like It Hot

Managing Pending Papers 63

Managing Nonpending Papers 70

Managing Activities 71

Managing Routine Information 76

**CHAPTER 6**    **Maintaining the System**    79

Seize the Day

Keeping Up with Current Filing: The Four-Step
    Maintenance Plan    81
Weeding Out Unneeded Papers    89
Moving Inactive Records    90
Protecting Vital Documents    90
Closing Up and Gearing Up at Year's End    93

**CHAPTER 7**    **Organizing Writing Projects—
Start to Finish**    95

From Here to Eternity

Setting Up an Ideas Category    97
Setting Up Writing Project Categories    101
Setting Up an Ongoing Project Category    108
Tracking Your Writing Projects    109
Dealing with Rough Drafts    112
Dealing with Dropped Projects    113
Restoring Order When Projects Are Completed    113

**CHAPTER 8**    **Marketing Manuscripts**    115

Great Expectations

Targeting Buyers for Your Manuscripts    117
Submitting Manuscripts for Publication    120
Tracking Your Marketing Efforts    122
Tracking Your Credits and Clips    128
Dealing with Rejection    132

**CHAPTER 9**    **Tracking Financial Records**    135

The Burden of Proof

Understanding the Value of Keeping Clear
    Financial Records    137
Setting Up Financial Categories    139
Managing Paperwork Related to Incoming Cash    147
Managing Paperwork Related to Outgoing Cash    151
Tracking Your Income and Expenses    153
Managing Tax-Related Paperwork    162

**CHAPTER 10**    **Bringing Computers into the System**    167

Brave New World

Buying or Upgrading a Computer System    170
Learning How to Use a Computer System    176
Naming Computer Files    177

Organizing Computer Files: The Five-Step
    Computer Management Plan                         177
Maintaining Computer Files                              182
Creating and Storing Forms on the Computer              184
Preparing for Computer-Related Disasters                184

**CHAPTER 11  Designing the Workspace**                 187
Room at the Top
Reviewing Your Current Office Layout                    190
Creating Space to Work                                  194
Creating Space to File                                  199
Creating Space for Storage                              202
Planning Your Revised Office Layout                     204

**CHAPTER 12  Understanding Organizational Styles**     207
As You Like It
Understanding Type                                      210
Determining Your Type                                   210
Applying Type to Organizational Style                   216
Getting Filing Help from Other Types                    217
Factoring in Other Influences                           226
Learning More About Type                                226

**Epilogue**                                            229
This Side of Paradise

**RESOURCES**  Paper Management                          233
Psychological Type                                      233
Writing                                                 234
Writing Reference                                       234
Words                                                   234
Grammar                                                 235

Index                                                   237

# ACKNOWLEDGMENTS

We appreciate the following readers of the manuscript: David Abrahamson, Lynette Ayers, Diane Dorff, Michael Fine, Dean Hallford, Jean Heroux, Sandra Hirsh, Jean Kummerow, Ann Lewis, Larry McDonald, Bill Young, and others. Their suggestions brought clarity and perspective to the book.

Our gratitude to several hundred fellow writers who revealed with candor and wit how they deal with their piles of paper. These writers opened their offices, cubbyholes, and file drawers, and told all.

Thanks to Jack Lindstrom, for his lighthearted cartoons, and to Al Papas, for his clear, specific graphics.

Sincere thanks to our editor, Barbara Anderson, for her insight, focus, and expertise.

# INTRODUCTION

**T**HIS book is for people who write.

Everyone writes—memoirs, articles, proposals, speeches, reports, grants, curricula, cookbooks, ad copy, novels, stories, how-to books, manuals, letters, memos, and more.

*File . . . Don't Pile!*® *For People Who Write* is not about *how* to write. Honing writing skills is up to you. Bookstores have plenty of how-to books on learning the basics, developing plots and characters, and finding agents.

This book focuses on the *paper* writers deal with.

Heaps of it.

The examples in this book feature writers of one kind or another, whether they write as a vocation or as an avocation. But anyone can use this filing system, as more than a hundred thousand buyers of Pat Dorff's original *File . . . Don't Pile!*® already know. Even Ludwig van Beethoven would have found solace in this System. Wherever he lived (he made eighty moves in Vienna alone) the gifted composer was prone to piling.

Books and sheets of music would be scattered in every corner . . . the hurried outline of a new quartet . . . the slumbering embryo of a symphony . . . a printer's proof awaiting release. Personal and business letters would litter the floor. . . . Only when something simply could not be found, despite hours, days, even weeks of searching, [he would complain] *"Ja, ja! . . .* What a disaster! Nothing stays where I put it; everything has to be moved somewhere else; I am a fool to put up with it . . ."

Your workspace may be in an office building or in your home. The main question is: How do you cope with paper? One seasoned writer tells how she deals with it:

My clipboard, my three-hole punch, and my oversize rubber bands
. . . *they* keep my life together.

Another writer complains:

Who would think you could lose a project folder within thirty-
square feet? Trust me. It happens to me all the time.

The File . . . Don't Pile!® System is not a stopgap measure. It shows
how to *plan* first, then *act* as you organize your writing papers.

You won't implement the ideas in this book in a single breathtaking
session. Work at your own pace. After all, how long did it take you to
accumulate the mess? Once you establish the foundation, your system
can grow with your writing.

No more paper landslides. No frantic searches. No repeated research.
No missed deadlines.

Your ability to organize paper affects your writing productivity, efficiency, and success. Most writers dream about having more space and
more time. *File . . . Don't Pile!® For People Who Write* can help you set
up a filing system to maximize the time and space you do have so you
can do what you do best—write!

# CHAPTER 1
# Facing the Mess

## My Side of the Mountain

Jean George

SOME writers are born organized. You can drop in on them unannounced. They'll greet you with a smile and lead you into a writing nook from the pages of *Office Beautiful* magazine. Their offices are orderly; their desks spotless.

But other writers? They rush to bar the door. If you get through, you'll see paper everywhere—blocking windows, carpeting the floors, spilling from file drawers. These writers plaster lamp shades with Post-its™, bury desks under a mélange of books, and balance drafts atop computer monitors. "What do you mean *mess?*" they ask. "This *is* my system!"

Do you have the uncanny ability to misplace papers without leaving your desk chair? Do you jam file folders until they bulge, clip piles of articles, and save every draft? Is your side of the mountain poised for a paper avalanche? Unless you get a thrill from archaeological digs, you need a filing system—one that works now and keeps on working.

Two kinds of clutterers are reading this book. Some clutterers pile papers from floor to ceiling, from front door to back. The key word is *on.* Papers can be found *on* the desk, *on* the floor, *on* the chair, *on* any flat surface. These writers operate according to the out-of-sight, out-of-mind theory. Here's how one writer describes it:

I can't trust myself to put things in their proper places. I'll forget to do something important if I file it away. The result is "urgent action" papers piled all over every available horizontal surface.

Other clutterers stockpile just as much paper, but it's well hidden. Their key words are *in, under,* and *behind.* Papers are stashed *in* closets, *in* drawers, *in* filing cabinets (piled, not filed), or tucked *under* desks and *behind* doors. These clutterers have the world fooled. People think they're organized. Only they know the truth.

At the heart of any filing system is this key question: Can you find what you need when you need it?

Quick! Take this One-Minute Mess Test. Can you put your hands on these hypothetical papers or records?

- The source for the quote you're using
- Notes from your editor's last call
- Your computer's service record
- The article you saved on anecdotes
- The rejection slip with the supportive note
- The summary of this month's expenses
- The marketing records for a specific manuscript
- The idea you scribbled on a napkin last week

How did you do? How fast can you retrieve essential information from your current files? One writer admits:

I wasted more than an hour sorting through six copies of a seven-page manuscript to see which of the forty-two sheets belonged to the latest revision.

For her, that was the last straw. What finally makes *you* say, "This is it! The mess *has* to go!"? Just plain sick of the clutter? Moving, getting married or divorced, changing jobs, running out of space, celebrating a landmark birthday? Whatever pushes you into action, you want a solution and you want it now. There's no quick fix, but there *is* a secret to paper control.

## Learning the Secret to Paper Control

You may have heard this highly touted "secret" to paper control: Handle a piece of paper only once.

It's a great idea. Do it as much as possible. But the one-decision-per-paper solution isn't always practical. You may touch the same piece of paper several times as you review and revise your work.

The *real* secret to managing paper is based on this simple fact. You have only two types of paper:

*Pending* papers     *current, active*, and/or *frequently used*
*Nonpending* papers     *past, inactive*, and/or *seldom used*

4

"Big deal!" you say. "Pending . . . nonpending? That doesn't help me get my papers organized." Step back. Look at all the paper you're responsible for, both professional and personal. Every scrap of it is either pending or nonpending.

> The secret to paper control is knowing which papers are *pending*, which papers are *nonpending*, and how and where to organize both kinds.

To see how this applies to you, do the following exercise. Make three columns on an 8-½-by-11-inch sheet of paper. Label the left-hand column "Documents," the center column "Action(s)," and the right-hand column "Deadline." Now, in the Documents column, randomly list ten to fifteen types of paper piled on your desk. Next to each document note what kind of action(s) you need to take and the deadline for each action. For example:

| DOCUMENTS | ACTION(S) | DEADLINE |
|---|---|---|
| CHAPTER FOR NEW BOOK | REVISE 1ST DRAFT | BY FRIDAY |
| CONTRACT | TALK TO LAWYER | ASAP |
| PROJECT PROPOSAL | FINISH AND MAIL | END OF MONTH |
| RESEARCH DATA FOR COMPLETED ARTICLE | FILE | WHENEVER |
| MAGAZINE ARTICLE NOTES | FINISH RESEARCH; WRITE DRAFT | IN TWO WEEKS |
| CATALOG | FILE | WHENEVER |

Just as in the example, some of the papers on your list are probably pending and some are nonpending. That's why your desk looks like a hodgepodge with nonpending papers scattered among your pending papers. This book will show you how to organize both types of paper and how to stay caught up. You'll use this exercise again. Paper-clip it into your book until you get to Chapter 5.

Ready to get started? Turn to Chapter 2 for step-by-step directions.

# CHAPTER 2
# Digging In

## The Charge of the Light Brigade

Alfred, Lord Tennyson

**W**HAT happens when "Dig-In-and-Do-It Day" arrives? Here's a typical scenario: Fired with determination, you roll up your sleeves and charge—like the Light Brigade—into the mounds of paper. You divide them into neat piles: everything for your current manuscript goes here; research notes go over there; financial papers go in one spot; rejection slips and marketing information go in another.

Sort. Sort. Sort.

Then, you look at the clock. The day is half gone and you have to rush to an appointment.

What happens to these tidy stacks?

1. They stay separated at first, but gradually get buried by new paperwork heaped on top of them . . . or . . .
2. They're piled in one big crisscrossed stack until your next straightening blitz.

Ring true?

After this big sort, you may *feel* as though you've made progress toward getting organized. The place may *look* neater. But you still don't have a workable filing system.

This approach isn't new. Calius Patronius, consul of the Roman Empire, had the same problem with his scrolls in 47 B.C.:

. . . we tend to meet any new situation by reorganizing, . . . creating the *illusion* of progress while producing confusion, [and] inefficiency . . .

Before you move in like a whirling dervish and create the illusion that you're organizing, pause. Think about a construction project. How

do the workers accomplish their jobs? Do they storm in with hammers and nails and slap up walls willy-nilly? Of course not. The workers follow a blueprint, an overall plan that provides direction.

With the File ... Don't Pile!® System, you plan first and *then* act. This chapter helps you create a sense of direction—your own filing blueprint.

Some consultants advise you to start your organizing binge with today's paperwork, the "do now" papers piled on your desk. "Worry about the rest later," these organizers say. This Band-Aid® approach might work if all you want is a quick fix, but such short-term remedies fall apart in a few days or weeks. Getting organized without a long-range blueprint is nothing more than temporary tidying.

If you want a long-term solution to your current mess, don't ignore your backlog of papers. From the beginning, include in your plan *all* the types of writing papers that you deal with. That way your system will work six months or even six years from now.

How *do* you create your plan—especially if papers are scattered in could-be-anything piles and stacked in drawers? If you've been coping with a quasi-system or have information in your files that should have been tossed years ago, where do you begin?

Start with the Five-Step Organization Plan (see page 10). Steps 1 through 3 are the "thinking" steps that help you create your filing plan. Plan *before* you act. You can keep functioning with your regular work during these steps without disrupting your present system. When you complete the first three steps of the Five-Step Organization Plan, you'll have a road map and know where you're headed. The last two steps are the "action" steps. When you physically start to move your paperwork, you won't have to ask, "Where should this folder go?"

## Tackling the Paper Mess:
## The Five-Step Organization Plan

**STEP 1: MINIMIZE.**
**DISCARD & CONSOLIDATE YOUR PAPERS**

Step 1 is *to discard unneeded papers and consolidate loose papers.* The best way to start is to minimize the mess, especially if paper clutter is everywhere. Toss unneeded papers and corral the loose ones so you'll know what to include in your filing plan.

Like some writers, you may think each piece of paper you touch is sacred. Vital. A keeper. Not so. Files grow crowded with old and inactive materials. Purge and merge. You may make some surprising discoveries—long-forgotten papers, similar headings filed in several drawers, empty folders, maybe even those car keys you lost last year.

First, label six boxes: **TOSS, FILE, ACTION, QUESTIONS, CLIP**, and **TRANSFER**. These boxes are *not permanent*. (At least they aren't supposed to be!) They're a means to an end to help you get organized.

Then go through loose papers or folders piled on flat surfaces and stacked in drawers. Scan folders filed in cabinets. Briefly review each loose paper or folder and take one or more of the following actions:

1. Throw away papers you no longer want or need in the **TOSS** box. (Recycle them if you can.) Don't get bogged down in deep cleaning. Weed out papers on which you can make an instant "toss" call—outdated materials, duplicate copies, and papers from past interests. Use the questions listed on pages 14–15 to help you evaluate whether a paper is "saveworthy." You can still discard papers during other steps in the Five-Step Organization Plan. You're bound to discover other items to be tossed as you create your filing plan.

2. Refile any folders that already have "homes" in your current filing system, if you have one. If material doesn't have a clear place in your files or if you don't have a system, put the folders in random order in one section of a drawer or box labeled **FILE**. You'll arrange the folders in a logical order later. Create additional **FILE** boxes as needed.

3. Group loose papers containing similar information into temporary folders—manila or hanging. Pencil in a working heading such as *Recession* or *Undervalued Stocks*. Add the folders to your current filing system or put them in random order in one section of a drawer or box labeled **FILE**.

4. Store critical don't-lose papers that need immediate attention in a *temporary* box labeled **ACTION**, or use small baskets or brightly colored file folders. Later in Chapter 5, you'll learn efficient ways to organize these action papers.

5. Park papers you can't readily identify in the **QUESTIONS** box. Step 4: Centralize (page 24) discusses what to do with these problem papers.

6. Put all magazines, newspapers, or other materials you want to cut out into the **CLIP** box. *Don't reach for your scissors!* If you stop to clip information, you'll lose momentum.

7. Put materials you need to transfer out of your workspace—borrowed materials and papers you plan to pass onto others—into the **TRANSFER** box. Put a Post-it™ Note on each item to remind you where it's headed.

8. Make sure headings reflect what is really in existing folders. If a heading reads *Writers*, but the folder actually contains only research on F. Scott Fitzgerald, pencil in the more specific heading.

9. Consolidate duplicate folders only if the duplication is obvious and you can merge folders *quickly*.

Work steadily, not stopping to read, write, file, or clip material. Everything should fit into one of the boxes *or* your wastebasket. How long it takes you to sort and toss your loose papers and folders, depends on how much you have. When you finish, look at your workspace. The wood grain on the desk has resurfaced. No more piles of paper are stuffed in drawers or leaning against the walls. Your filing system isn't in place yet, but you have restored some order to your workspace and you're ready to move on to Step 2.

## Key Questions for Evaluating Paper
••••••••••••••••••••••••••••••••••••••••••••••••••••••••••••••••••••••••••••

Use these questions to help you to decide whether a paper is worth keeping (so you can *seize control of paper you already have*) or acquiring (so you can *control your paper intake*).

1. **Do I WANT it?** Savers beware! You may be tempted to say, "Of course I want it! I want everything that's in print." Be ruthless. Instead of automatically keeping a flyer for a mystery writers' conference, ask: "Will this fit into my schedule? Can I afford this? Am I even interested in writing mysteries?" Be discriminating, too, about "freebie" materials available at conventions.

2. **Do I NEED it?** Some papers you definitely need: tax documents, computer warranties, contracts, bank records. But do you really need bulky drafts of every piece you've written? When the project is complete, a single final copy will suffice. If you can't dispassionately toss old drafts, time-date them for later disposal or save only unused portions for the future.

3. **Will it ADD SOMETHING NEW?** Does the information provide a fresh viewpoint or lend a new perspective to what you already have? If it doesn't break any new ground, it's redundant and doesn't belong in your files. Do you really need another article on Abraham Lincoln's trademark stovepipe hat if such information is already well-documented in your reference files?

4. **Is it USEFUL to me?** As your interests change, so should the papers you save. If you've shifted from writing drama reviews to writing sports commentary, a piece on "Innovative Set Designs" is no longer of value to you. What's useful to one writer may not be to another. If you teach writing classes, keep your students' needs in mind. Multiple copies used for handouts could warrant space in your files.

5. **Can I FORESEE A USE for it?** Creative types tend to say: "You never know . . . I *might* need it someday." This rationale can choke a system. If you're a teacher-turned-writer, data on new elementary math principles might come in handy if you decide to combine your teaching and writing skills to develop math materials. To justify saving a piece of paper, be sure you could actually use the topic in the future.

6. **Is it TIMELY?** Some information is time-dated and some is timeless. Topics, particularly those in scientific fields, quickly lose their relevance. Fast-moving changes may make information obsolete in months. On the other hand, tips and strategies for instilling a love for reading in children often span the decades.

7. **Is it QUALITY information?** What is quality to you may not be to someone else. Use the watchwords *reliability, accuracy*, and *validity* to assess quality. Evaluate the author's credentials. Build your own quality control system to decide what is saveworthy.

8. **Can I OBTAIN IT ELSEWHERE?** Do you stockpile every *Scientific American* ever published? Libraries index and preserve back issues on microfilm. If you're sixty-seven miles from a major library, however, you'll save a half-day's journey if you can refer to your own copy.

   You don't need to be the official "Keeper of all the Keys." Can a colleague, a department, or an office supply the information? "I feel more secure with my own copies," you say. "Then, I *know* that I've got the information." (Never mind that what you want is buried in the basement and would take a miracle and a crowbar to find.)

## STEP 2: GENERALIZE.
## IDENTIFY YOUR PAPERS

Step 2 is to *identify what papers you have to organize.*

In Step 1 you corralled loose papers into temporary folders and refiled papers in your present system, if you have one. This gave you a good idea of what papers you've accumulated. But unless you have a photographic memory, it's easy to forget what's hidden away in drawers and boxes. You need an inventory.

Don't be tempted to plunge right into filing. Your inventory is the most important planning tool you'll use. It shows the kinds of current and past paperwork you actually have. You won't itemize every single piece of paper; you'll just make a *general* list of the folders in file drawers and those you put in the boxes labeled **FILE**.

You can create your Inventory List manually or on your computer. A computerized list allows you to work faster as you complete Step 3 of the Five-Step Organization Plan (see page 18). Your list may be one or several pages long, depending on the amount of papers you have to organize. Here's how to inventory:

1. Sketch your workspace, noting the places where you file papers. Assign a letter to each location. For example, label the file cabinet *A*, the desk *B*, the boxes in the corner *C* and *D*, and the bookshelf *E*. Then assign a number to each space in the location. Since the desk is *B*, make the desktop *B1*, and the four desk drawers *B2*, *B3*, *B4*, and *B5*.

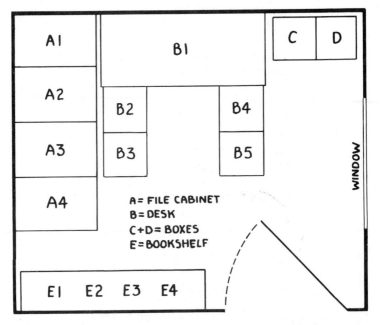

2. Inventory each drawer or box. Remember, *generalize*. List only the words written on the tabs of the folders, not each paper within the folders.
   - To inventory manually, list the contents on a pad of paper or clipboard
   - To inventory on a computer, ask another person to work with you—one reads off the tab headings of folders, while the other keys them in
   - Another option is to record the list manually, then enter it into the computer

3. At the top of each page of the inventory put this information: Inventory List, date of inventory, file location code, and location. It will look like this:

```
                    INVENTORY LIST
                       (Date)

        A1   File Cabinet/First Drawer
```

4. Set up three columns on each page of your Inventory List. Make the first two columns narrow, the third, wide. For now, leave the first column blank. In the second column, key in the file location code—for example, A1. In the third column, key in the working heading from the tab label of the folder. Keep the heading brief so it fits on one line. A partial Inventory List for a writer may look like this:

```
                    INVENTORY LIST
                       (Date)

        A1   File Cabinet/First Drawer

        A1   Plot development
        A1   Fiction Writer's Association Directory
        A1   Short story ideas
        A1   Writing magazine lists
        A1   Dialogue
        A1   Viewpoint
        A1   Survey
        A1   First draft of "Molly on the Overland Trail"
        A1   Flashbacks
        A1   Miscellaneous
        A1   Five Senses
```

5. Continue the inventory process for each file location until you have a complete list of all your folders.

*TIP:* Keep the urge to purge to a minimum as you inventory. If you decide to toss a folder of papers, eliminate the tab heading from your Inventory List. But if you find many items that should be tossed, go back to Step 1. Purge and then do the inventory.

## STEP 3: CATEGORIZE.
## GROUP SUBJECTS BY CATEGORY

Step 3 is to *group your subjects into broad categories.*

To understand why, try this: Make an alphabetical list of all the people you've ever known in your entire life.

Overwhelming, isn't it? That's because the mind doesn't work alphabetically. You don't think of friends, relatives, and colleagues in alphabetical order! Your brain links and connects ideas—you categorize *like* ideas.

If pressed to alphabetize the names of everyone you know, you'd simplify the job by dividing the names into manageable groups—"Lab," "Department," "Organizations," "School," "Family," and others. Then you'd organize the names within these groups.

It's the same with paper. Many people already file by categories. They separate their papers into four or five groups, including one very large one dubbed **MISCELLANEOUS**. If a paper doesn't fit into one of the other main categories, it's tossed into **MISCELLANEOUS**, a useless catchall category.

To divide your paperwork into groups logical for your needs, do two things:

1. Create an Areas/Categories List
2. Code your Inventory List

### *Create an Areas/Categories List*

Divide your writing papers into broad areas and categories. *Areas* act as large umbrellas under which two or more categories can fit. *Categories* are groups of several related subjects or topics. The Areas/Categories List on page 19 shows five broad filing areas many writers use and typical categories for each area. This isn't meant to be a definitive list of writers' categories. Use these suggestions as a springboard to discover your own.

```
                     AREAS/CATEGORIES LIST


MANUSCRIPTS AREA

IDEAS
PROJECTS  [for short writing projects]
MOLLY ON THE OVERLAND TRAIL  [a longer writing project]
DROPPED PROJECTS
PAST PROJECTS


MARKETING AREA

MARKETING LEADS
MARKETING ACTION
CREDITS AND CLIPS


FINANCIAL AREA

INCOME
EXPENSES
MONTHLY TRANSACTIONS
TAXES


REFERENCE AREA

WRITING MECHANICS REFERENCE
WRITING SKILLS REFERENCE
WRITING GENRES REFERENCE
BUSINESS AND LEGAL REFERENCE
MARKETING REFERENCE
GENERAL REFERENCE


ADMINISTRATIVE AREA

FORMS
WRITING BUSINESS  [your company name]
GROUPS/ORGANIZATIONS  [one folder per group]
WRITERS' ASSOC. OF AMERICA  [many folders if more involved]
MASTERS
```

Areas and categories give your papers "homes." If the historical society sends you information on stagecoach routes for a book you're writing on the Overland Trail, it goes into the *MANUSCRIPTS AREA* in the category, **MOLLY ON THE OVERLAND TRAIL**. When a bill arrives, it goes into the *FINANCIAL AREA* in the category, **EXPENSES**.

Some writers have difficulty thinking of potential categories for their papers. Others have trouble nailing down categories because they come up with so many options that they can't settle on one.

**19**

*I get confused about what category to use when I file. Does information about speed skating go into an Olympics folder or with my story about winter sports?*

If this problem sounds familiar, here are some suggestions to help you determine your own filing areas and categories. Start with the categories you already have. Then add other viable groups in which your writing papers can "live." Your categories should reflect *your* work and activities.

Study your Inventory List. It identifies the kinds of papers you have. Ask other writers or colleagues what categories work for them.

Brainstorm by clustering. Here's an example of one editor's **COMPANY NEWSLETTER AREA** with possible categories and subjects:

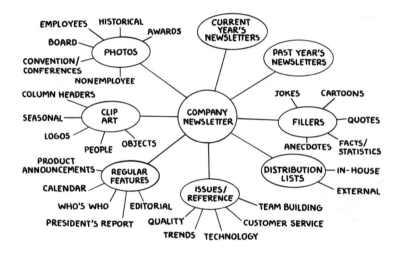

Once you know your categories, how do you find the most appropriate and descriptive names for them?

*I know which pigeonhole to put these papers in. I just don't know what to call it!*

Here are tips to help you name your writing categories:

- **Use a name that communicates the purpose of the category.** The category name should indicate what kinds of papers live there. For example, use **QUERY LETTERS** instead of **LETTERS**.

- **Use *your* jargon to name the categories.** Choose terms meaningful to you. Most writers call their **IDEAS** category, **IDEAS**. It's a clear, straightforward name. But one writer calls this category her **FLUFF FILE** and even draws clouds all over the folders. Who cares? It's her category.

- **Use standard category names within a department or in team writing efforts, when consistency is important.** If one person refers to a category as **DONATIONS**, another calls the same category **DRIVES**, and a third, **MONEY SOURCES**, confusion reigns. Instead, jointly agree on a uniform name, such as **FUND-RAISING**.

- **Use a brief heading in naming the category.** Shorter names, rather than wordy headings, focus the user more quickly. For example, use **CHILD DEVELOPMENT** rather than **HUMAN GROWTH AND DEVELOPMENT IN YOUTH**.

Take the time now to work out your areas and categories. After you complete your list, develop a short code for the category names so you won't always have to write them out. Use two, three, or four letters that plainly identify the category. Which is clearer, MK or MKT/L for **MARKETING LEADS**? Here are some examples of various writing categories and possible codes:

| *Code* | | *Category* |
|--------|---|------------|
| CR | = | **CREDITS AND CLIPS** |
| IDEA | = | **IDEAS** |
| GRP | = | **GROUPS/ORGANIZATIONS** |
| MKT/L | = | **MARKETING LEADS** |
| WS/R | = | **WRITING SKILLS/REFERENCE** |

### Code Your Inventory List

So far you have created two lists—an Inventory List (to show what papers you have) and an Areas/Categories List (to show where your papers can "live"). You may be eager to start *physically* moving papers and file folders. Hold back! Here's why.

Remember the construction workers? Can you imagine their building a house without a blueprint and having to move the wall studs each time the owner decides to relocate a doorway? Just as the blueprint comes first, you decide on the categories where your subjects will live *before* the actual filing begins.

Here's how. "Marry" your Inventory List and Areas/Categories List to create a *Coded* Inventory List. Assign categories to the items on your Inventory List by coding each one. Your Inventory List then becomes the Coded Inventory List.

Scan your Areas and Categories List to decide in which category each item on your Inventory List best fits. Put the code for that category in the left column of the Inventory List to show where the item will be housed. If you decide a given subject fits better in a different category, the Coded Inventory List lets you easily change your mind. Just erase and recode the item.

Here are some other codes you may want to use:

- **Question Mark (?).** If you're not sure in which category the item belongs, put a ? (question mark) by it. Don't be concerned about problem papers. They'll fall into place as the System builds.

- **Sort (SORT).** If you need to review and divide up papers in the folder, put the code SORT by the item. Use this code for all those ubiquitous folders labeled "Miscellaneous."

- **Toss (TOSS).** Put the code TOSS by the item if you think it can be discarded. There's no need to toss at this point—just code your list. Later you can review and toss those items.

- **Transfer (TR).** Put the code TR by the item, if you need to *transfer* it to someone else or to another location. Transfer items might include papers to give to someone else or papers to transfer to another department or to central files.

If you have many items to transfer to a particular location or person, assign an identifiable code—DEPT for Department or CT for Catherine Thomas, for instance. Using this code, rather than TR for TRANSFER makes it easy to separate these items from other TR items. If nonwriting papers, such as personal items, are mixed in with your writing materials, code them PER. You can create a plan for your personal files another time. (For personal and household categories, see Pat Dorff's original *File . . . Don't Pile!*®.)

The illustration below shows a sample Coded Inventory List with the category codes marked in the left column.

```
               CODED INVENTORY LIST
                     (Date)

             A1   File Cabinet/First Drawer

WS/R         A1   Plot development
GRP          A1   Fiction Writer's Association Directory
IDEA         A1   Short story ideas
MKT/L        A1   Writing magazine lists
WS/R         A1   Dialogue
WS/R         A1   Viewpoint
?            A1   Survey
OT           A1   First draft of "Molly on the Overland Trail"
WS/R         A1   Flashbacks
SORT         A1   Miscellaneous
WS/R         A1   Five Senses
```

**STEP 4: CENTRALIZE.**
**GATHER YOUR PAPERS**

Step 4 is to *gather like papers together in one location.*

Centralizing means grouping related papers so you can set up your files by categories. In Step 3 you decided in which categories you want your papers to live (your Coded Inventory List.) But your papers won't beam themselves magically into their new categories. Now you're ready for action.

Use the Post-it™ Note Approach to centralize your subjects. Here's where your *prefiling* planning pays off.

### *The Post-it™ Note Approach*

1. *Get Post-it™ Notes.* You'll need several packages of 1½-by-2-inch Post-it™ Notes.

2. *Label and affix Post-it™ Notes.* Start with one of your file drawers or the boxes you created, and the Coded Inventory List for that location. This list shows the category you assigned to each file folder.

   Label a Post-it™ (writing at the top, the sticky edge at the bottom) with the code for that item from the Coded Inventory List. Then flag the folder with the Post-it™. Do this with each folder in the drawer or box.

   If you marked an item on the Coded Inventory List with a "?," quickly thumb through the folder's contents. If you can determine its category, label the Post-it™ Note with the appropriate code. If not, label the Post-it™ Note with a "?." You'll deal with the "?" items later during Step 4.

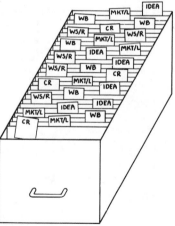

3. *Group file folders into like categories.* At a glance, scan the drawer and see which folders have matching Post-it™ labels. Pluck out those folders and put them in one section of the same drawer if there is space. If there isn't enough space, establish a section in another drawer or in an empty box.

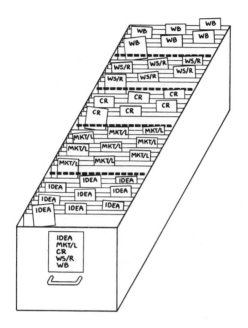

The Coded Inventory List is an essential guide for centralizing your papers. Now you need another list that will show you which papers "live" together in each category. Here's when a computerized inventory is a real plus. Some software can reorder a computerized list with a sort command. Presto, a Sorted List!

If you did your Inventory List manually, the sorting process is slower. You'll need to find all items with the same code on each page of your Coded Inventory List, and to rewrite these items on separate sheets of paper—one category per page. Create separate pages for items coded "?," "SORT," "TOSS," and "TR."

The next page shows an example of the sorting process. The first list is a Coded Inventory List for a file cabinet drawer, location A1. The second list is a Sorted List for the category WS/R, **WRITING SKILLS/ REFERENCE**. All boldfaced items on the first list that are coded WS/R have been pulled out and put on the Sorted List for the WS/R category.

(Note that items coded WS/R from other drawers appear on this list, too.)

```
                    CODED INVENTORY LIST
                         (Date)

            A1    File Cabinet/First Drawer

WS/R        A1    Plot development
GRP         A1    Fiction Writer's Association Directory
IDEA        A1    Short story ideas
MKT/L       A1    Writing magazine lists
WS/R        A1    Dialogue
WS/R        A1    Viewpoint
?           A1    Survey
OT          A1    First draft of "Molly on the Overland Trail"
WS/R        A1    Flashbacks
SORT        A1    Miscellaneous
WS/R        A1    Five Senses
```

```
                        SORTED LIST
                         (Date)

WS/R   WRITING SKILLS/REFERENCE FILE

WS/R        A1    Plot development
WS/R        A1    Dialogue
WS/R        A1    Viewpoint
WS/R        A1    Flashbacks
WS/R        A1    Five Senses
WS/R        A2    Character development
WS/R        A2    Openers/leads
WS/R        A2    Endings
WS/R        A2    Tension
```

With your papers sorted and gathered, you can deal with the sticklers, those problem items you put in the **QUESTIONS** box and the folders identified as "?" on the Sorted List. Most people find that problem papers either fit into one of their established categories or can be discarded. Use the eight questions on pages 14 to 15 to help you decide what to toss. Scan your Sorted Lists for logical categories for the rest. If you find like papers without homes, create a new category.

When you finish Step 4, euphoria sets in. Centralizing can *almost* come under the category of fun!

What next? Move on—you're ready for Step 5.

STEP 5: ORGANIZE

**STEP 5: ORGANIZE.**
**FILE YOUR PAPERS**

Step 5 in organizing your papers is to *set up files for your papers*.

Caution: Complete Steps 1 through 4 before you start the actual filing process.

Some people, determined to get organized, buy out an office-supply store. They invest in filing cabinets, folders, and plastic gizmos, thinking that these tools are the solution. Without a plan, they're throwing money at the problem. If you've done this, you've skipped directly to Step 5, bypassing four very important steps.

It's not the containers that matter. It's the system *inside* that counts. Getting organized doesn't have to cost much money. Here's all you need to begin:

- *Paperdex™*. Any filing system worth its salt has a key. The key to the File . . . Don't Pile!® System is the Paperdex™. This index saves you and others using your files time and frustration.

  The beauty of the Paperdex™, whether done manually or by computer, is that you don't have to rummage through all the files in your brain or office to remember where you filed something. With the Paperdex™, you put your memory on the index. File information and forget it until you need it.

  Guess what happens without a Paperdex™? If you're the only one who knows how your system works, you do all the retrieving. That may be fine if you work alone and have a perfect memory. But if you ever forget a file location, or if your files may be used by others, the Paperdex™ index unlocks the whole system.

**27**

- *File folders.* You don't need any special folders to set up the File . . . Don't Pile!® System. But third-cut manila folders and hanging folders are recommended. (Choose letter- or legal-size folders.)

   The next two chapters describe how to use the Paperdex™ and file folders to set up files for each of your categories.

## Persevering with Your Plan

No one can possibly file every paper in each category simultaneously. You need to set priorities. Which category takes precedence over the others? Do you need to organize your **CREDITS AND CLIPS** first or your **MARKETING LEADS**? What's in worse shape—**MOLLY ON THE OVERLAND TRAIL** or **IDEAS**?

To get started, print this heading at the top of a sheet of paper:

### PRIORITIES LIST

Now list the order in which you want to organize all your categories. Give the messiest or most urgent categories top priority. Folders with some semblance of order can wait while you clean up the rest of the chaos. One writer listed his smallest category first so he could feel a sense of accomplishment. You decide. Be sure to include *every* category on your Priorities List. It's your plan of attack!

How long will it take *you* to complete the five steps? That depends. How much paper do you have? How many interruptions? Do you have any help? What is your commitment to the project? (Yagottawanna!)

What's your organizational style? Have you ever wondered why organization is so natural for some people and so challenging for others? To learn how personality type affects the way people file . . . or pile, read Chapter 12.

Don't let anyone fool you. Filing takes time. Everything may not get filed in one day, even if your papers are centralized. If it's taken you ten years to accumulate the treasures, it's going to take some time to organize them. But, whatever your pace, don't feel guilty about it. You're getting started and you *can* do it!

I work full time as a curriculum writer. On the side I write a weekly newspaper column, as well as free-lance articles, and teach writing workshops. It took me six months to do the five steps, but they've helped me move forward bit by bit.

As you dig out from under your piles of paper, you'll find material you didn't even remember you had. You won't be alone. The chief of the Library of Congress's manuscript division once came across a handwritten draft of the Bill of Rights. This working copy had been missing for 196 years!

Once your categories are established and your papers centralized, you're ready to file! With your Priorities List in hand, you're focused. Read on for the how-to's of filing.

# CHAPTER 3
# Setting Up
# a Filing System

## A Light in the Attic
Shel Silverstein

..........................................................................................

IMAGINE receiving a big box for your birthday. You open it eagerly and find a "what's-it" you've been wanting for years. The problem? The gizmo has hundreds of pieces, but no instructions.

Likewise, you may be looking at the ten boxes of papers and folders you just categorized and centralized, but you're not sure how to organize them. What *system* do you use to file *your* papers so you won't forget where they are?

A confident secretary in a cartoon explains to her boss, "It's an easy system. I file everything under 'P' for Papers."

You want your system to be simple, but not that simple. This chapter provides the "light in your attic"—step-by-step instructions for setting up your categories.

The File . . . Don't Pile!® System offers two ways to file your papers. One, the A–Z Method, is used for broader categories with numerous subjects. The other, the Prefix Method, is ideal for more narrow categories with fewer subjects. Both use a combination of letters and numbers—an alphanumeric code—and have two key features:

- The Paperdex™
- Coded file folders

Many filing systems use some kind of index. The File . . . Don't Pile!® System index is called the Paperdex™.

Each category has a Paperdex™ on which you record codes, subjects, and cross-references. The Paperdex™ serves as Control Central for the category and provides instant access to the correct file you need at any given time. (To get preprinted Paperdexes™, use the order form at the back of the book.)

The statistics are in:

**When you file papers by category, by color, and by the alphanumeric method of filing, you cut your retrieval time by 50 percent. When you also use the Paperdex™, you cut retrieval time by 70 percent!**

Here's how both methods work and when to use them for your writing categories.

## Using the A–Z Method

If you have a lot of paper to be filed in a category, or if the category is likely to expand, use the A–Z Method of filing.

> *Rule of thumb:* Use the A–Z Method when you have a category that has **35 or more subjects**.

Usually the only categories requiring the A–Z Method are large reference categories such as a **GENERAL REFERENCE** category that includes background information on a variety of topics you may write about.

### THE A–Z PAPERDEX™

An A–Z Paperdex™ is a set of specially lined 8½-by 11-inch forms. Each page represents one letter of the alphabet except the last, which covers X, Y, and Z. Use a permanent fine-tip marking pen to print a letter of the alphabet in the upper right-hand corner of each page.

All A–Z Paperdex™ pages have three columns. The left-hand column is labeled **SUBJECT**, the center column **SEE ALSO**, and the right-hand column **SEE**. This chapter explains how to use the **SUBJECT** column. The **SEE ALSO** and **SEE** cross-reference columns are covered in Chapter 4. On the next page is a partial page from an A–Z Paperdex™.

You'll need one A–Z Paperdex™ for each broad category you create using the A–Z Method. File the Paperdex™ in a center-tab folder at the front of the category. Use a colored folder, which will be easy to spot and will act as a divider when you file more than one category in the same drawer.

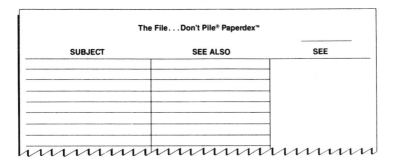

## THE A–Z CODE

The A–Z Method Code has two parts—a single letter and a number.

*The Letter:* Base the code letter on the first letter of the *subject.*

Subjects beginning with "A" use an A in their codes. For example, in a **GENERAL REFERENCE** category, "A" subjects—*Appalachia, Appaloosas*—would have a code starting with A. "B" subjects—*Bosnia, Bach*—would have a code starting with B, and so on.

If a subject heading consists of more than one word, base the code letter on the first letter of the first word. For example, use "E" for *Endangered Species.*

*The Number:* Base the code number on the order in which you add new subjects.

Paper doesn't come into your life in alphabetical order. The subjects in your files don't need to be alphabetized either. In the example below, the subject, *Amish,* was the third "A" topic filed, so its code is A103. *Soccer* is listed before *Saskatchewan* because information for that subject was filed first.

A101 Appalachia          S101 Saxophones
A102 Appaloosas          S102 Soccer
A103 Amish               S103 Saskatchewan

For some people, a longer number, such as 101, 102, and 103, is easier to read. This is a personal preference.

## TAB POSITIONS FOR THE A–Z METHOD

Before creating the folders, decide how you want the tabs of the folders lined up in the file drawer. Although the tabs are arranged left to right, there are two ways to stagger them. You decide which one you prefer.

The first way is to alternate the tab positions within each letter. In the illustration below left, each letter uses the left-tab position for all 101s, center tab for 102s, right tab for 103s, and so on.

For a cleaner look, designate one tab position for each letter as shown in the illustration below right. All A codes use left-tab, all Bs use center-tab, and all Cs use right-tab positions. Go back to the left tab for D codes, and so on.

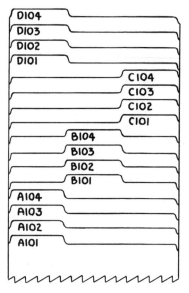

## DRY RUN: START YOUR ENGINES!

Give the A–Z Method a dry run with the following example: A radio commentator who writes vignettes on San Francisco history has collected many articles and notes about little-known facts. Assume that he has started a **SAN FRANCISCO HISTORY** category. He has an article called "Four-Generation Family Seeks Fortune in Cookies."

He decides that *Chinatown* makes sense as the subject for that article, and flips to the "C" page of his Paperdex™. Since *Chinatown* is not yet listed, it will become the sixth subject on the "C" page and be coded C106. Next he takes these three quick steps:

## Step 1: Mark the Paperdex ™

In the left-hand column of the "C" page of the Paperdex™, print the code (C106) first, then the subject (*Chinatown*). (See below.) **Always work in pencil in your Paperdex™**. Remember, you don't necessarily list subjects alphabetically. You can quickly scan a whole column for a specific subject.

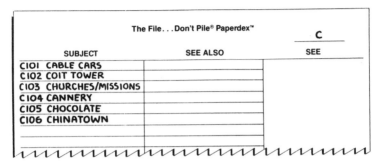

The File...Don't Pile® Paperdex™

**C**

| SUBJECT | SEE ALSO | SEE |
|---|---|---|
| C101 CABLE CARS | | |
| C102 COIT TOWER | | |
| C103 CHURCHES/MISSIONS | | |
| C104 CANNERY | | |
| C105 CHOCOLATE | | |
| C106 CHINATOWN | | |

## Step 2: Mark the Item

Print the code (C106) in the upper right-hand corner of the article about fortune cookies. That way, it will be easy to re-file. If you don't want a code splashed across the top, print it on the back of the item.

## Step 3: Label the File Folder

Choose the correct tab position (left, center, or right) for the code C106. Print the selected code and subject on the tab or on a self-stick tab label with a permanent felt-tip pen. Or you can generate labels with a typewriter or computer. Another option is to print the subject in pencil if you think it may change.

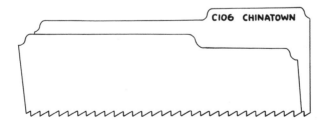

C106   CHINATOWN

The A–Z Method lets you file large quantities of related information within a single category. But what if all the paperwork for a committee is crammed into one or two bulging folders? In that case you won't have enough different headings to justify setting up files by the A–Z Method. The solution? The Prefix Method.

## Using the Prefix Method

For categories with a limited number of subjects, use the Prefix Method. Most people find they use the Prefix Method for far more categories than they use the A–Z Method.

> *Rule of thumb:* Use the Prefix Method when you have a category that has **35 or fewer subjects.**

### THE PREFIX PAPERDEX™

The Prefix Paperdex™, is a specially lined 8½-by-11-inch form. In the upper right-hand corner of the Prefix Paperdex™, print the prefix code assigned to a category, such as GRP for the **GROUPS/ORGANIZATIONS** category. Below it, print the name of the category: **GROUPS/ORGANI-ZATIONS**. See the example below.

| The File...Don't Pile® Paperdex™ | | GRP<br>GROUPS/ORGANIZATIONS |
|---|---|---|
| **SUBJECT** | **SEE ALSO** | **SEE** |
| GRP-1 CRITIQUE GROUP | | |
| GRP-2 LAKE REGION WRITERS NETWORK | | |
| GRP-3 M.W.A. | | |
| GRP-4 INDEPENDENT PUB. ASSN. | | |
| GRP-5 TOASTMASTERS | | |
| GRP-6 CHAMBER OF COMMERCE | | |

Like the A–Z Paperdex™, the Prefix Paperdex™ has three columns: **SUBJECT, SEE ALSO,** and **SEE**. (**SEE ALSO** and **SEE** are detailed in Chapter 4.)

You'll need one Prefix Paperdex™, a single form, for each category you set up using the Prefix Method. File the Prefix Paperdex™ in a center-tab folder at the front of the category. Use a colored folder, which will be easy to find and will act as a divider between categories filed in the same drawer. Here is a partial page from a Prefix Paperdex™ for a category called **IN LEFT FIELD** for a monthly baseball newsletter.

| | The File...Don't Pile® Paperdex™ | LF |
| | | LEFT FIELD |
| SUBJECT | SEE ALSO | SEE |
| --- | --- | --- |
| LF-1 EDITORIALS | | |
| LF-2 FEATURES | | |
| LF-3 CLIP ART SERVICES | | |
| LF-4 THEMES | | |
| LF-5 SPOTS | | |
| LF-6 CALENDARS | | |

## THE PREFIX CODE

The Prefix Method code has two parts—prefix letters and a number. While the A–Z Method uses a single letter of the alphabet, the Prefix Method code uses a combination of letters.

> *The Prefix Letters:* Base the prefix code letters on the letters that best represent the name of the *category*.

The prefix letters remain the same for every subject within the category. A prefix code of two to four letters works best. The sorting codes that you used in Step 3 of the Five-Step Organization Plan (page 18) may also serve as prefix letters, or you may think of a clearer code. A prefix can be an abbreviation or a short word. Choose letters that communicate what the category is. Some examples of category codes might be:

| | | |
| --- | --- | --- |
| IDEA | = | **IDEAS** |
| SWG | = | **SCREENWRITING GUILD** |
| WS/R | = | **WRITING SKILLS/REFERENCE** |
| WG/R | = | **WRITING GENRE/REFERENCE** |
| MKT/L | = | **MARKETING LEADS** |
| EXP | = | **EXPENSES** |

> *The Number:* Base the prefix code number on the order in which you add new subjects.

In most cases, the order doesn't matter. The prefix code is the common thread that holds the category together. The illustration below shows how easy it is to scan for specific subjects even though they aren't alphabetized. You can also choose to sequence subjects geographically or chronologically. If, for example, you teach a seminar called Basic Grammar, you could organize the course materials in the order you use them.

Use a short number—1, 2, 3, and so on—since the prefix usually has two to four letters in the code.

| SUBJECT | The File...Don't Pile® Paperdex™ SEE ALSO | **BG** BASIC GRAMMAR SEE |
|---|---|---|
| BG-1 WHY GRAMMAR? | | |
| BG-2 COMMON BLOOPERS | | |
| BG-3 PARTS OF SPEECH | | |
| BG-4 ORAL ERRORS | | |
| BG-5 USAGE | | |
| BG-6 REVISION/PROOFREADING | | |

**TAB POSITIONS FOR PREFIX METHOD**

As with the A–Z Method, decide before you create the folders how you want the tabs of your folders to line up in the drawer—in a staggered or straight line.

With the staggered approach, use a left tab for the first prefix code and repeat the left, center, right tab sequence for the entire category.

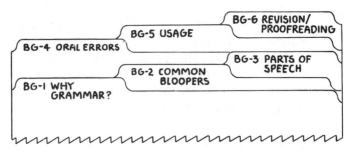

40

With the straight-line approach, use the same tab position—left, center, or right—for the entire category.

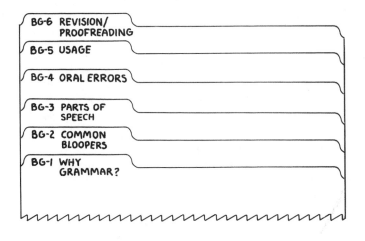

BG-6 REVISION/
PROOFREADING

BG-5 USAGE

BG-4 ORAL ERRORS

BG-3 PARTS OF
SPEECH

BG-2 COMMON
BLOOPERS

BG-1 WHY
GRAMMAR?

### DRY RUN: START YOUR ENGINES!

Give the Prefix Method a dry run with the following example: File a pamphlet for the Compu-Write Graphics Company in the **WRITING BUSINESS** category. The WB Paperdex™ for this category already has five subjects, but when you scan this list you see that the pamphlet for this word-processing service doesn't fit under any of these headings. You need to create a new subject, such as *Graphics Services*. Follow the same three steps used in the A–Z Method.

### *Step 1: Mark the Paperdex™*

In the left-hand column of the Paperdex™, print the new prefix code (WB-6) first, then the new subject (*Graphics Services*). (See below.) **Always work in pencil in your Paperdex™.**

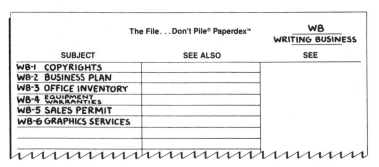

The File...Don't Pile® Paperdex™

WB
WRITING BUSINESS

| SUBJECT | SEE ALSO | SEE |
| --- | --- | --- |
| WB-1 COPYRIGHTS | | |
| WB-2 BUSINESS PLAN | | |
| WB-3 OFFICE INVENTORY | | |
| WB-4 EQUIPMENT WARRANTIES | | |
| WB-5 SALES PERMIT | | |
| WB-6 GRAPHICS SERVICES | | |

### *Step 2: Mark the Item*

In the upper right-hand corner of the pamphlet, print the code (WB-6.) This makes it easy to refile.

### *Step 3: Label the File Folder*

Choose the correct tab position (left, center, or right) for the code (WB-6). Print the selected code and subject on the tab or self-stick tab label with a felt-tip pen. Or you can generate labels with a typewriter or computer. Another option is to print the subject in pencil if you think the topic might change.

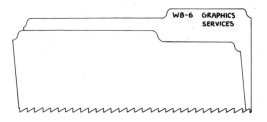

#### VARIATION OF THE PREFIX METHOD

You may have some categories, such as **PUBLISHERS, CATALOGS**, or **EDITING CLIENTS**, which would make sense to alphabetize. To maintain continuity within your filing system, use a variation of the Prefix Method. The Prefix-Alphabetic Method uses only the letters, no numbers, in the Prefix Code. The prefix letters provide instant category recognition and make refiling easier. Use the straight-line approach to arrange the tabs. The following page shows examples of a **CATALOGS** category and an **EDITING CLIENTS** category.

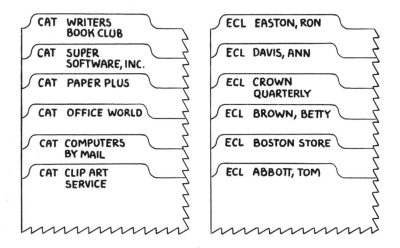

## Deciding Which Method to Use

How do you decide which method, the A–Z or Prefix, is right for a particular category? The answer depends on how much material you have or will collect. Remember the rules of thumb:

Use the *A–Z Method* for categories having **35 or more subjects**.

Use the *Prefix Method* for categories having **35 or fewer subjects**.

Narrow the focus of your categories so that related materials are more clearly defined and accessible. Topics in the broad category **WRITING REFERENCE**, for example, could range from plots and pacing to punctuation and plays. When divided into three mini-categories, the subjects become more focused. For example:

**WRITING SKILLS**      Dialogue, viewpoint, climax, openings/
endings, characterizations . . .

**WRITING GENRES**      Poetry, mystery, nature, travel, sports . . .

**WRITING MECHANICS**      Grammar, usage, synonyms, spelling,
syntax . . .

## Why Use a Pencil?

Why this emphasis on entering data in Paperdexes™ for both the A–Z and the Prefix Methods in pencil? Here's why: In a library, when a book is permanently removed, not only is the book pulled from the shelves, but also the title is deleted from the catalog. So it should be with the subjects in your files.

If you eliminate the subject *Childhood Nutrition* from your **HEALTH AND NUTRITION** category, you should not only discard the information but also delete the subject heading from the Paperdex™. Using pencil makes this easy to do. If you leave the code in place, HN-3 is now available for another new topic, such as *Carbohydrate Loading*, in **HEALTH AND NUTRITION**.

One writer said it best: "My file headings are chameleons. They keep changing." You might also think of a better way to word a subject after you have entered it in the Paperdex™. Because you've used pencil, you can erase the old heading and enter the new one.

## Color-Coding

Color plays a major role in your filing system. It serves as an instant identifier and differentiates categories within the file drawer. Use color to signal something meaningful to you, such as yellow for the **IDEAS** category. Let color work for you!

There are only so many colors in the rainbow. Use a color chart like the one on the next page to plot out which colors you'll assign to each of your categories. Knowing which categories will "live" next to one another in the drawer also helps you choose your color scheme. You may need to repeat some colors. Notice how all project categories are color-coded blue while marketing-related categories are green.

| RED | YELLOW | BLUE | GREEN | PURPLE | ORANGE | PINK | BLACK | BROWN | GOLDENROD |
|---|---|---|---|---|---|---|---|---|---|
| EXP WB WG/R | TRANS IDEA | TAX PR DPR PPR OT | INC MKT/L MKT/A MKT/R | WM/R | WS/R | GRP WAA | CR REF | MAS FM | BL/R |

One way to color-code is with colored manila and hanging file folders. This is eye-catching, but pricey. You can introduce color with the standard green hanging folders by using colored plastic tabs, colored interior folders, or colored labels. Here are several ways to incorporate color, starting with the least expensive option:

---

### Color Options for File Folders

- *Manila folders:* Put a strip of color on the top edge of the tabs with a colored permanent-ink marking pen.
- *Manila folders:* Use colored adhesive labels.
- *Green hanging folders with manila interior folders:* Use colored adhesive labels on the manila folders and corresponding colored plastic tabs on the hanging folders.
- *Green hanging folders with colored interior folders:* Use corresponding colored adhesive label plastic tabs.
- *Colored hanging folders with manila interior folders:* Use corresponding colored adhesive labels and colored plastic tabs.
- *Colored hanging folders with colored interior folders:* Use corresponding colored adhesive labels and colored plastic tabs.

---

Remember the One-Minute Mess Test in Chapter 1? How fast can you find a paper *when* you want it? With the File . . . Don't Pile!® System's A–Z Method and Prefix Method, the answer is easy: **You can find most papers in sixty seconds or less!** You may be thinking, "Sure I can find my papers that fast . . . as long as you ask me right after I've filed them!"

If filing papers and promptly forgetting where you put them sounds familiar, read on. Chapter 4 deals with cross-referencing and its memory-jogging **SEE** and **SEE ALSO** clues.

# CHAPTER 4
# Cross-Referencing Files

## The Road Not Taken

Robert Frost

**H**AVE you ever said, "I finally got it all together, but where did I put it?" You file something under *Anxiety* in January and look for it under *Worry* in December, and wonder why you can't find your "buried treasures."

Many creative writers can reel off a half-a-dozen ways to say the same thing. Forced to choose one subject heading when they file, they look down "the road not taken" and, like Robert Frost's traveler, wish they could wander in both directions. Here's the catch. The same term may not always come to mind when they file and when they retrieve.

Writers try all kinds of memory joggers. One novelist says:

> I used to lose ideas until I began jotting them down in a notebook. Now I have trouble finding the ideas in the notebook! But they're in there someplace.

Another problem writers face when filing is knowing where to put papers when they relate to several categories. One common solution is to put six copies in six places! "Perfesser" Cosmo P. Fishhawk, the blustery journalist owl in the "Shoe" cartoon strip, tried that method. Here's what he mumbled about his experience with this copycat trap:

> [This] is an important document. I made one copy for my personal file . . . one copy for my home office records . . . one copy for my lawyer, one for my accountant, a copy for the boss . . . and one copy inserted into the middle of this pile of rubbish on my desk. I need to keep one copy where I can always find it.

Cross-referencing to the rescue! Think of a cross-reference as an arrow on a road sign. It points the way and saves you hours of bumpy-road detours.

This chapter covers three kinds of cross-references:

**SEE** cross-references
**SEE ALSO** cross-references
**REMINDER** cross-references

Here are three important reasons for cross-referencing:

* To nudge your mind into remembering
* To direct others to information
* To cut down on duplicates

## Using SEE Cross-References

The **SEE** column says, "Hey, do you want information on such and such a subject? Then, look under (or **SEE**) this subject." The purpose of the **SEE** column is to give *location*. It tells you where to go—nicely, of course.

List **SEE** cross-references in the right-hand column of the Paperdex™. Notice that on a Paperdex™, the **SEE** column is unlined. The absence of lines signals that **SEE** is independent—it has no connection with the other two columns on the Paperdex™.

You don't read straight across the Paperdex™ page. In the illustration below, you don't read, for instance, from *Helium Balloons* straight across to *Hong Kong*, or from *Harvard University* straight across to *Hodgkin's Disease*. These subjects are not related.

The **SUBJECT** column on the left is where you list subjects for which you have actual folders containing information. No folders exist for subjects you list in the right-hand **SEE** column. You may wonder, why bother listing them?

The File...Don't Pile® Paperdex™

**H**

| SUBJECT | SEE ALSO | SEE |
|---------|----------|-----|
| H101 HELIUM BALLOONS | A105 | HONG KONG - F101 |
| H102 HULL HOUSE | | HOCKEY - S104 |
| H103 HARVARD UNIV. | | HODGKIN'S DISEASE - C105 |
| H104 HOLOGRAMS | | |
| H105 HATS | C106; F108; S103 | HIBERNATION - B102 |
| H106 HOROWITZ, VLADIMIR | M111; P108 | HENRY, MARGUERITE - A107 |

The **SEE** column helps you remember where you interfiled information. Even though you may not have a whole folder of information on the subject *Hong Kong*, you may have tucked one or two items in with material on the subject *Far East* in folder F101. Or you may have stashed an obscure chart on hibernation you picked up at a nature center in with the subject *Bears* in folder B102. Again, the Paperdex™ on page 50 illustrates these cross-references.

There are three times when you'll want to list subjects in the **SEE** cross-reference column:

- When you can refer to a subject in more than one way
- When you can interfile a subject within a broader subject heading
- When you interfile an obscure item and could forget its location

**HOW TO ENTER SEE CROSS-REFERENCES IN THE PAPERDEX™**

Start the list of **SEE** cross-references at the top of the **SEE** column. Remember, *always work in pencil.* Indicate only the subject being cross-referenced and the code of the folder where you can find the topic. Add subjects to the list as needed. Don't worry about alphabetical order. A quick glance shows you all the topics listed.

Here are examples of the three cases when you'll use **SEE** cross-references:

> **When you can refer to a subject in more than one way.**

What is *Appetizers* to one food editor is *Hors d'oeuvres* to another. The subject *Hot Dishes* becomes *Casseroles. Candy* becomes *Confections*, and so on. The key? **Choose the term YOU'LL be most likely to look under when wanting specific information.**

The File ... Don't Pile!® System doesn't lock you into predetermined subject headings. Use the term that's best for you.

Then list alternative terms in the **SEE** column in case you forget, or for when another person uses your files.

If you usually refer to *Openers* as *Beginnings*, then *Beginnings* is the term to use in the **SUBJECT** column. Make a note in the **SEE** column that says "Openers, WS/R-4" in case you forget which term you chose.

Once you decide what a subject heading will be, write it and its code in the **SUBJECT** column. Then ask yourself, "Will I remember this subject heading next month or next year? What else might I call it? A quick notation of alternative headings in the **SEE** column saves you endless search time.

| | The File...Don't Pile® Paperdex™ | WS/R WRITING SKILLS REFERENCE |
|---|---|---|
| SUBJECT | SEE ALSO | SEE |
| WS/R-I QUALIFIERS | | OPENERS – WS/R-4 |
| WS/R-2 CLICHÉS | | COLLOQUIALISMS – WS/R-2 |
| WS/R-3 OVERSTATEMENT | | HYPERBOLE – WS/R-3 |
| WS/R-4 BEGINNINGS | | |
| WS/R-5 RHYTHM | | |
| WS/R-6 IRONY | | |

**When you can interfile a subject within a broader subject heading.**

If you have only one or two papers on a subject, it's not practical to file them in their own folder, unless you know the subject might expand. A favorite response is, "I'll just stick this stuff in with such and such." Whenever you tuck a single item in with another subject, you interfile.

Sometimes you may interfile information within a related subject that has a broader scope. Other times you may interfile papers within subjects that seem to make sense at the time. Will you remember two or three months later that you interfiled information about Jesse James in

| | The File...Don't Pile® Paperdex™ | CRIM CRIMINALS IN HISTORY |
|---|---|---|
| SUBJECT | SEE ALSO | SEE |
| CRIM-I MAFIA | | JESSE JAMES – CRIM-2 |
| CRIM-2 MIDDLE BORDER BANDITS | | ZORRO – CRIM-3 |
| CRIM-3 HIGHWAYMEN | | |
| CRIM-4 MEDIEVAL | | |
| CRIM-5 WHITE COLLAR | | |
| CRIM-6 WESTERN | | |

the subject *Middle Border Bandits* in your **CRIMINALS IN HISTORY** category? You will if you make a note in the **SEE** column. See illustration on page 52.

Perhaps you write science textbooks and have a reference category called **INSECTS**. You have only one or two articles on the monarch butterfly and have filed information about these long-distance travelers under the subject heading *Migration*.

If you use the Prefix Method for the **INSECT** category, the subject may appear as INS-3 *Migration*. File the article in INS-3 and cite the cross-reference in the **SEE** column as "Monarch Butterflies"—INS-3.

| The File...Don't Pile® Paperdex™ | | INS INSECTS |
|---|---|---|
| SUBJECT | SEE ALSO | SEE |
| INS-1 SOCIAL INSECTS | | MONARCH BUTTERFLIES-INS-3 |
| INS-2 PROTECTIVE COLORATION | | |
| INS-3 MIGRATION | | |
| INS-4 LIFE CYCLES | | |
| INS-5 MATING HABITS | | |
| INS-6 BENEFITS | | |

If you use the A–Z Method for the **INSECTS** category and M105 is the code for *Migration*, file the article in M105. Then in the **SEE** column on the M page of the **INSECTS** category Paperdex™, cite the cross-reference as "Monarch Butterflies—M105."

| The File...Don't Pile® Paperdex™ | | M |
|---|---|---|
| SUBJECT | SEE ALSO | SEE |
| M101 MOTHS | | MONARCH BUTTERFLIES-M105 |
| M102 MATING HABITS | | |
| M103 MANDIBLES | | |
| M104 METAMORPHOSIS | | |
| M105 MIGRATION | | |
| M106 MIMICRY | | |

Sometimes it's the little scraps of paper or unusual items that get lost in the shuffle. One writer says:

I don't have trouble keeping track of the obvious—neon-yellow manuals and thick reports. It's the odd-duck stuff I don't know what to do with.

It doesn't matter if it has been six weeks or six months since a mystery writer filed a chart called "Perfect Poisons." Cross-references make retrieving materials a snap.

With a Prefix Method **MYSTERY** category (MYS), the writer files this chart under the subject *Murder Methods*, MYS-2. In the **SEE** column, she writes the cross-reference, "Perfect Poisons—MYS-2."

The File. . .Don't Pile® Paperdex™

**MYS**
**MYSTERY**

| SUBJECT | SEE ALSO | SEE |
|---|---|---|
| MYS-1 ALIBIS | | PERFECT POISONS- MYS-2 |
| MYS-2 MURDER METHODS | | |
| MYS-3 HIDEOUTS | | |
| MYS-4 BODY DISPOSAL METHODS | | |
| MYS-5 MOTIVES | | |
| MYS-6 DISGUISES | | |

A prolific mystery writer may have more than thirty-five reference topics. He needs to use the A–Z Method for his **MYSTERY** category. He could interfile the article, "Perfect Poisons," within the subject *Murder*, M104. On the "P" page of the Paperdex™, he'd write the cross-reference, "Perfect Poisons—M104."

The File. . .Don't Pile® Paperdex™

**P**

| SUBJECT | SEE ALSO | SEE |
|---|---|---|
| P101 PALACE LAYOUTS | | PERFECT POISONS-M104 |
| P102 PISTOLS | | |
| P103 PATHOLOGY | | |
| P104 POLICE | | |
| P105 PLOTS | | |
| P106 POLTERGEISTS | | |

The subjects for some items may not be obvious. Retrieval is slower because you can't remember where you filed them. A reference article about a luxury-train excursion, "All Aboard the Scottish Express," might be filed under *Scotland* or *British Isles* or *Excursions*. When you want it, all that may come to mind is "train ride." Those words weren't even in the title of the article. Is it lost? No. The **SEE** cross-reference prevents this.

Here's how a Prefix Paperdex™ for a **GREAT BRITAIN** category might appear:

| SUBJECT | The File. . .Don't Pile® Paperdex™ SEE ALSO | GB GREAT BRITAIN SEE |
|---|---|---|
| GB-I BRITISH ISLES | | TRAIN RIDE – GB-2 |
| GB-2 SCOTLAND | | |
| GB-3 EXCURSIONS | | |
| GB-4 ISLE OF SKYE | | |
| GB-5 WALES | | |
| GB-6 CASTLES | | |

You can put your hands on information quickly, even if it's an obscure item. Make as many notations in the **SEE** column as you wish. The **SEE** cross-references nudge your memory and provide easy access if others use your file.

## Using SEE ALSO Cross-References

The **SEE ALSO** cross-reference says, "Hey, look! There's *more* information about this subject if you **SEE** *ALSO* these related topics." The important word is ALSO.

**SEE ALSO** is used for only one reason:

> When you can find *additional* information about a subject in other files.

**SEE ALSO** cross-references are easy to list.

## HOW TO ENTER SEE ALSO CROSS-REFERENCES
## IN THE PAPERDEX™

List **SEE ALSO** cross-references in the center column of the Paperdex™ on the same line as their related subjects. The **SUBJECT** column and the **SEE ALSO** column are directly related. That's why they are linked with horizontal lines.

Just cite the codes for the related subjects in the **SEE ALSO** column. Writing in the subject name takes up too much space on the line. *Always work in pencil.*

Here's an example. If you are researching biographical subjects from the revolutionary war era, you might have a reference category called **REVOLUTIONARY WAR** with the code REV. Your REV Paperdex™ lists REV-3 *Clothing* in the **SUBJECT** column. Because you do extensive research, you also have a *Uniforms* folder, REV-6.

If you look up *Clothing* in the Paperdex™ below, you'll find a notation on the same line in the **SEE ALSO** column to check REV-6. You know right away that *more* related information about clothing is filed in REV-6. And if you look up *Uniforms*, the **SEE ALSO** column leads you to REV-3.

| | SUBJECT | SEE ALSO | SEE |
|---|---|---|---|
| REV-1 | SPEECH | | |
| REV-2 | MAPS | | |
| REV-3 | CLOTHING | REV-6 | |
| REV-4 | HOUSING | | |
| REV-5 | FOOD | | |
| REV-6 | UNIFORMS | REV-3 | |

The File. . .Don't Pile® Paperdex™    REV REVOLUTIONARY WAR

Whenever you list a topic in the left-hand **SUBJECT** column of a Paperdex™, think about whether you have also filed related materials under other subjects. If you have, enter their codes in the **SEE ALSO** column.

# Cross-Referencing from One Category to Another

Remember how the journalist in the "Shoe" cartoon strip made six copies of an important document and filed it in six different places? A better solution would be to file the information in one category and cross-reference it. Use **SEE** and **SEE ALSO** cross-references both within a single category and between categories.

If your file uses the Prefix Method, the letters of the prefix code will identify which category to look in. If you have set up more than one category using the A–Z Method, indicate which category you're referring to. A104 may be *Alligators* in a **SCIENCE** reference category or *Arkansas* in a **GEOGRAPHY** reference category. *Always work in pencil.*

The Paperdexes™ below show examples of how **SEE** and **SEE ALSO** cross-references can direct you to other categories for information whether you use the A–Z Method or the Prefix Method.

| The File...Don't Pile® Paperdex™ | | A |
|---|---|---|
| SUBJECT | SEE ALSO | SEE |
| A101 APPALACHIA | | ABORIGINES – A106 |
| A102 APPALOOSAS | | |
| A103 AMISH | IDEA-8; | ASTHMA – PR |
| A104 ALLIGATORS | | "SNEEZING AND |
| A105 AIDS | | WHEEZING IN |
| A106 AUSTRALIA | | SAN DIEGO" |

| The File...Don't Pile® Paperdex™ | | BL/R |
|---|---|---|
| | | BUSINESS AND LEGAL REFERENCE |
| SUBJECT | SEE ALSO | SEE |
| BL/R-1 BUSINESS PLANS | BL/R-8 | COLLABORATION |
| BL/R-2 COPYRIGHTS | | BL/R-6 |
| BL/R-3 NETWORKING | MKT/R-9 | |
| BL/R-4 LEGAL ISSUES | | DISABILITY BL/R-5 |
| BL/R-5 INSURANCE | | PLAGIARISM BL/R-2 |
| BL/R-6 CONTRACTS | | |

## Using REMINDER Cross-References

Some cross-reference information is too detailed to fit on your Paperdex™. The third type of cross-reference, the **REMINDER** cross-reference, is a note that you store right in the file folder. **REMINDER** cross-references can save you time, money, and space.

Use a **REMINDER** cross-reference:

- When information is in a book or manual
- When an item is too big for a file folder

**REMINDER** cross-references go directly into file folders, not in the Paperdex™. Jot them on 3-by-5-inch cards or on a sheet of paper taped inside the folder.

Here are examples of the two cases when you'll use **REMINDER** cross-references.

---

### When information is in a book or manual.

---

You probably have favorite passages, poems, or ideas in books on your shelves relating to papers in your writing files. You won't rip the books apart. You need a way to correlate the information in your books with your filed materials.

For instance, if you happen across a fine example of a ballad, such as Henry W. Longfellow's "The Wreck of the Hesperus," and want to remember which book it is in, put a **REMINDER** cross-reference under the subject *Ballads* in your **POETRY** category.

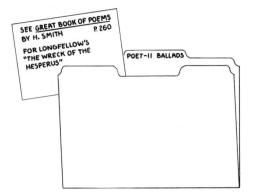

## When an item is too big to fit into a file folder.

If an item, such as an envelope of information, thick brochure, or map, is too bulky to fit into a standard folder, two options are to use box-bottom folders or to sandwich the item directly behind the folder it should be filed in. Be sure to write the proper code on the item.

Some materials are just too big to fit into a filing cabinet. With **REMINDER** cross-references, you can store large items on a shelf or in a closet, and still find them easily. A person who writes math curriculum materials could have the following **REMINDER** cross-reference in a middle-grade math reference file:

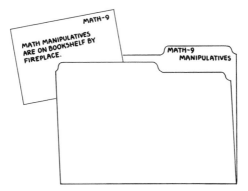

When should you write **SEE**, **SEE ALSO**, or **REMINDER** cross-references?

> **Add cross-references when you think of them—as you *file*
> or when you *retrieve*.**

Whose brain can recall all the tiny bits of information about what's located where? Remember the old Chinese proverb, "Even faded ink is better than the worst memory." Write it down! The more cross-referencing you do, the more valuable your files will be. The longer you're a writer, the more extensive your cross-references will become.

You won't have to remember every minute detail because your cross-references are on the job. If you ghostwrite, collaborate, or teach writing with another person, cross-references make it easy for someone else to find information.

Now that you know how to organize your files, it's time to learn where to house them. Chapter 5 shows you how to identify which papers are pending and which are nonpending, so you can apply the real secret to managing your papers.

# CHAPTER 5
# Managing Pending Papers

## Some Like It Hot

Billy Wilder & I.A.L. Diamond

**L**IKE some writers, you may think all papers are "hot"—*everything* is compelling. It all lands and stays on your desktop. But forgetting to act on papers is a chief concern, especially if you put them away.

Even though your files are set up, the constant barrage of new papers can boggle the mind. Incoming stuff mixes with papers of different ages, at different stages. If your modus operandi is "out of sight, out of mind," knowing what's really hot and what's not will help you manage the paper on your desk.

Remember the secret to paper control from Chapter 1:

> The secret to paper control is knowing which papers are *pending* (current, active, and/or frequently used), and which papers are *non-pending* (past, inactive, and/or seldom used), and how and where to organize both kinds.

## Managing Pending Papers

For many writers, dealing with action papers is an ongoing challenge. Even if you have only pending papers on your desk, the pile can still get deep. One writer refers to her desk as an incoming basket with a chair. She says:

> I'm afraid if I put something away, I'll forget it. My desk gets full and the bulletin board gets covered. Soon my whole *life* is pending.

So how do you handle the constant flow of "hot" papers? For starters, pull out the exercise you did in Chapter 1 (page 5) labeled,

Documents/Action(s)/Deadline

In the left-hand column, you jotted down a random list of papers piled on your desk. You wrote the action(s) to be taken on those papers in the center column. Notice how the deadlines listed in the right-hand column differ. Some actions require instant attention—"ASAP." Others, those less urgent, read "by end of month" or "whenever." Pending papers are not all created equal. Some papers are more pending than others.

Consider this analogy. A chef at a fine restaurant is preparing a seven-course feast for you. Ask yourself this question: Will the chef fix the entire meal using only the front burners? Probably not. The chef coordinates the meal so that each dish receives the attention it needs when it needs it. Some savory foods bubble on front burners. Others simmer on back burners.

Like the chef's stove, your desk is where the hot action takes place. Think of it as Action Central. Reserve any space on, in, or near your desk for action. Your pending papers, like the chef's pots and pans, need varying degrees of attention. But they don't all need to "cook on the front burner"—your desktop.

You have two types of pending papers:

*Front Burner Pending Papers*
- Demand immediate, "as soon as possible" attention or are used frequently
- Live in organizers *on the desktop*

*Back Burner Pending Papers*
- Require ongoing attention or are used on an as-needed basis
- Live in file drawers *in or near your desk*

Ask the following question about every pending paper that takes up residence on your desktop:

*When* does this pending paper need my attention?

If the answer is "immediately" or "soon," the paper belongs on the desk with other Front Burner Pending Papers.

If the answer is "on an as-needed basis" or "in the near future," the paper belongs in high-priority drawers in or near your desk with other Back Burner Pending Papers.

Take a closer look at the two kinds of pending papers—Front Burner Pending and Back Burner Pending.

### FRONT BURNER PENDING PAPERS

With the sweep of one arm, an executive in a cartoon brushes everything on his desk to the floor and announces to his secretary, "I've just cleared my desk, Emily, and I'm taking the afternoon off." Desktop management should be so easy.

Take a critical view of your desktop. Do you buy all the colorful, clever plastic bins on the market, then quickly load them up with stacks of papers? Syndicated columnist Ellen Goodman admits,

> My urge to get it together invariably . . . begins with the purchase of yet another organizer. You name it, I have bought it. Colorful files, multiple datebooks, calendars, a wall of pigeonholes, a thousand color-coded stickers, in-and-out boxes.

You can choose many kinds of organizers, including stackable letter trays, vertical sorters, memo racks, and step racks. Multicompartment space-savers with adjustable shelves and sorters can be attached to your desk to expand your work surface.

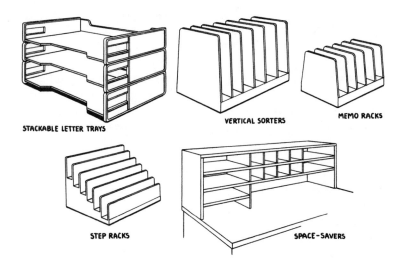

STACKABLE LETTER TRAYS  VERTICAL SORTERS  MEMO RACKS

STEP RACKS  SPACE-SAVERS

Any type of desktop organizer can make your desk look tidy—at least temporarily. But here's the critical question: Are your letter trays full—or are they *purpose*ful? Once you define the purpose of an organizer, it's less likely to fill up with miscellaneous papers. Such organizers all have compartments or slots. Here's how to pin down the purposes for those compartments.

Think of Front Burner Pending Papers as your "to be" papers. Fill in an action after the words "to be"—either *time* specific (To Be Completed by Friday) or *task* specific (To Be Called).

### Time Specific

- Group Action Papers by *like deadlines*: Ask *when* the action should be taken. For example, *Urgent* (means today), *A* (means this week), *B* (means by the end of the month), and *C* (means optional).

### Task Specific

- Group Action Papers by *like tasks*: Ask *what* type of action needs to be taken. For example, *To Be Called, To Be Written, To Be Reviewed*, and so on.

Whatever kind of organizer you choose, give each compartment in it a "to be" job.

Naming the compartment gives it power. Cartoon character Ziggy calls his in- and out-baskets by many names: "Agony/Ecstasy," "To Be/Not To Be," "Neither Here/Nor There." One writer keeps her desktop system simple with just two trays. The top one is "Hot," the other, "Not So Hot."

Before you're tempted to buy out an office-supply store to outfit your desk with an array of organizers ask yourself: What actions typically take place at my desk? Then purchase the desktop tools to manage them. One technical writer narrowed her actions to these eight:

1. To be given to (*name*)
2. To be acted on now
3. To be acted on soon
4. To be read now
5. To be filed
6. To be recycled
7. To be taken home
8. To be tossed

Clockwise, here are the organizers she uses and their related actions:

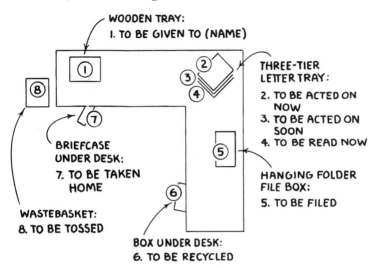

WOODEN TRAY:
1. TO BE GIVEN TO (NAME)

THREE-TIER LETTER TRAY:
2. TO BE ACTED ON NOW
3. TO BE ACTED ON SOON
4. TO BE READ NOW

HANGING FOLDER FILE BOX:
5. TO BE FILED

BOX UNDER DESK:
6. TO BE RECYCLED

BRIEFCASE UNDER DESK:
7. TO BE TAKEN HOME

WASTEBASKET:
8. TO BE TOSSED

Remember that papers in desktop organizers are there only for a short stay, not in permanent residence.

Two alternate methods of keeping track of Front Burner Pending Papers are a Tickler File and an Action Notebook.

### Tickler File

The Tickler File (also known as a Desk File or Day File) is an expandable book divided into two sections—1 to 31 for the days of the month and January to December. It's available in office-supply stores.

The Tickler File is *time driven*. Put action papers behind the dates you need to act on them. Although the tagboard pages don't have pockets, items don't fall out since the book is stored flat on the desk. You don't carry this around with you. Your success in using this tool

depends on whether you're the type of person who will check it each day for action papers.

Some people have difficulty using a Tickler File. In theory, it sounds good. They snap one up, thinking, "Finally! *The* answer for getting organized!" Their new Tickler File works for a short time; then they forget to look in it. Items filed in it are soon forgotten and "lost." The detailed structure and routine nature of the Tickler File contradicts the way some people operate. For many, the less-demanding Action Notebook is a better option.

### Action Notebook

The Action Notebook, a spin-off of the Tickler File, is *task driven*. Its big advantage is that it separates action papers by the kind of action they require rather than by the date they need to be acted upon.

You can create your own Action Notebook using a three-ring binder and as many pocket-page inserts as you need. Assign a task to each pocket (front and back) and stick labeled plastic tabs to the pocket pages. Arrange them in any order you wish. For example:

- To Be Done
- To Be Called
- To Be Given To (*Name*)
- To Be Read
- To Be Considered

Put papers in the pocket related to the type of action needed. Use your To Do List (see page 74) to keep track of what actions you need to follow up on. Use your Action Notebook to find the papers related to that task. When you complete the task, toss or file the papers.

The Action Notebook is a particularly useful tool if you need a portable means of rounding up action-related papers. Keep your Action Notebook handy.

I teach at three different sites. I kept leaving important stuff at the wrong place. Now my Action Notebook saves me.

## BACK BURNER PENDING PAPERS

Back Burner Pending Papers require ongoing or as-needed attention. They don't have to take up space on your desktop. But they need to be at hand so you can easily retrieve them.

To help you decide which papers are Back Burner, do this exercise: Make two columns on an 8½- by 11-inch sheet of paper. Label the left-hand column "Drawers In and Near Desk." Label the right-hand column "Drawers Away from Desk." In the left-hand column, list filing categories from which you frequently retrieve papers. In the right-hand column, list those you use less often and would walk across the room to retrieve. For example:

| *Drawers In and Near Desk* | *Drawers Away from Desk* |
|---|---|
| **CURRENT FINANCIAL** | **PAST FINANCIAL** |
| **CURRENT WRITING PROJECT** | **PAST WRITING PROJECTS** |
| **WEEKLY COLUMN** | **POTENTIAL WRITING PROJECT** |
| **FORMS** | **CRITIQUE GROUP** |
| **MARKETING** | **REFERENCE** |

The categories listed on the left are Back Burner Pending Papers. Those on the right, which don't require action or are seldom used, are nonpending. Paper-clip this exercise into your book until you get to Chapter 11. You'll use it again.

If you learn nothing else from this book, realize this: Your desktop and the drawers in and near your desk are prime real estate. Reserve this space for pending papers. You can do only so much in one day. File less urgent papers until you're ready to work on them. Write the task on a Master To Do List (see page 75) you keep in your Planning Notebook (see page 71). Let the list act as your reminder, not the piles of papers on your desk.

What about where to put small office supplies, such as a stapler, tape, Post-it™ Notes, scissors, pens and pencils, and paper clips? Use this rule of thumb:

| | | |
|---|---|---|
| **Often** | = | **Out** |
| **Seldom** | = | **Stashed** |

If you use items often, or daily, keep them out in the open on your desktop. If you use them seldom, once a week or less, keep them in the desk drawer. One writer uses a rotating caddy with pockets and hooks for storing such supplies.

Put your phone on the left side of the desk if you are right-handed, on the right side if you are left-handed. When the phone rings, you can grab the receiver and a pencil, and immediately start jotting down notes.

Take a hard look at your desktop. It's nice, even important, to have pictures of your favorite relatives in the office. But displaying the whole family tree takes up too much space. Cut the clutter. The fewer items on the desk, or the more compactly you organize them, the better.

## Managing Nonpending Papers

The term "nonpending" does not imply that the information is of lesser importance or of a lower quality. The nonpending status merely signifies activity level. Since nonpending papers have either low or no active usage, why bother keeping them? Here are six reasons:

- Legal
- Administrative
- Financial
- Reference
- Historic
- Potential

Papers related to projects in the idea stage are nonpending. You may wonder why they aren't considered pending since you need to take action on them. It's easy. Potential projects are nonpending because they aren't current, active, or frequently used.

I started writing a photography book six years ago and the partial manuscript nested in my top desk drawer that whole time. I still intend to do the book, but right now it's not a top priority. I finally moved the three-inch-thick folder to a less-used drawer across the room. It makes sense. When the time is right, I'll know where to find my manuscript.

Don't waste valuable active drawer space on noncurrent work. Keep it in a file cabinet or in a less-expensive storage box across the room or down the hall. Later, when you have the time or interest to act on it, you'll move it from your nonpending area to your pending area. If your office is in a business setting, you can transfer nonpending papers to a records center or an off-site storage facility.

## Managing Activities

In addition to writing, you may consult, speak, teach, and/or hold down a second job.

As demands on your time increase—professionally and personally—it's essential to develop a system for tracking responsibilities. Managing your time and activities is, in part, a paper affair. One writer, anxious that he remember appointments and critical "to-do" items, plasters himself with Post-its™. If a string around the finger isn't reminder enough for you, here are three tools that will help:

- Planning Notebook
- Goals
- To Do Lists

### PLANNING NOTEBOOK

A Planning Notebook does what its name implies: consolidates all of your plans—writing-related and personal appointments; scheduled events; upcoming meetings. It can also house your Master To Do Lists and notes.

I wrote a telephone number on the back of an envelope while I was taking a phone message. But where is it? I can picture the blue envelope in my mind, but I can't find it.

If you rely on notes stuffed in pockets or tacked up in myriad locations, it's easy to overlook commitments and forget details. When you use a Planning Notebook, it serves as an indispensable tool for organizing your time and activities.

Commercial planners are available in a variety of sizes and bindings. But you can create your own, tailored to fit your needs, for a fraction of the cost. Get a decent binder with rings mounted on the back cover so the pages will lie flat. The 6-by-9-inch and 8½-by-11-inch sizes are the most popular.

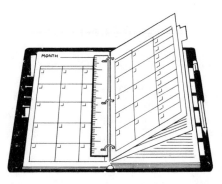

Put a calendar in the first section of the notebook. Reinforce the holes. Use a day-, week-, or month-at-a-glance version. It's your choice. (Some calendars have a Monday to Friday, Saturday to Sunday layout so that the weekend appears to the right of the page. Once you're used to this arrangement, you'll find it's a practical, logical approach for planning.)

Limit yourself to one calendar. It's the one time you need to mesh your writing and personal obligations. Otherwise this could happen:

I have a small calendar at work and a large family calendar on the kitchen door. Sometimes I forget to transfer information and miss a meeting!

Divide the rest of the Planning Notebook into as many sections as you wish. Designate each section for a specific action or interest. Here are examples. Adapt these suggestions to your needs or add your own.

- Master To Do List (professional)
- Master To Do List (personal)
- Goals
- Shopping
- Errands
- Calls
- Menu Plans
- People (discuss with)
- Library/To Read
- Critique Group
- Project Overview ⎫
- Ideas/Starters ⎬ (see Chapter 8)
- Words/Phrases ⎪
- Dialogue ⎭
- Addresses/Phone Numbers

Except for your calendar, addresses, and telephone numbers, most materials don't permanently "live" in your Planning Notebook. You'll just park information there temporarily until you use it or put it in your filing system. For instance, during a meeting at work:

- An idea strikes you for an article you could develop
- You receive an announcement you need to discuss at the next department meeting
- Someone mentions the title of a book you'd like to read

Open your planner to the related section and note the information.

Unless you're glued to your planner, you may still scribble notes on whatever paper is available. At least with a Planning Notebook in your life, loose jottings have a home base. And the habit of automatically dating papers lets you know how old they are so you can decide when to remove them from the Planning Notebook.

Your Planning Notebook is your lifeline. You don't want to misplace it! Here are three precautionary tips:

- Keep photocopies of key sections, such as your calendar, telephone numbers, and addresses
- Put your identification in the front cover
- Offer a reward in case you lose your Planning Notebook

Planning Notebooks are planners—not filing cabinets. Avoid stuffing action-related papers inside the front and back covers of your planner until the binding wheezes. Action-related papers belong in desktop organizers, in a Tickler File, or in an Action Notebook.

## GOALS

One writer, scrambling to meet last-minute deadlines before leaving on a two-week business trip to England, said, "My life is going faster than *I* am!"

Before you know it, another year has passed. Have you accomplished your writing goals? Did you write them down?

"Why bother with written goals?" you ask. "I know my goal—to publish!" It's not that simple. Written goals make you more committed and transform publishing hopes into reality. They dare you to change from thinking, "I could write a book," to actually writing one.

Goals create the framework for dividing grandiose writing plans into manageable chunks. You decide where you want to go with your writing and how much you can reasonably achieve in a given period of time. Goals remind you to, *"Do this!"* "Stay on track!" "Keep rolling!"

Since your projects and plans are unique, devise a goal form that works best for you. Keep your current copy in your Planning Notebook and check it frequently. The Writer's Tool Kit includes one example. (To order, see the back of the book.)

## TO DO LISTS

To Do Lists help you keep track of the actions you need to take. Whether your lists are casual or compulsive, view them as an extension of your memory.

There's no one right way to keep To Do Lists. Your approach depends on your organizational style. Some writers consistently use detailed, structured lists. Others use To Do Lists only when they're in a crunch. When the pressure eases, they function without one. One writer creates her To Do Lists on an as-needed basis:

When I know I'm going to spend the day working on Chapter 6, a To Do List is irrelevant. I'm glued to the computer for ten to twelve hours. If I have one or two calls I must make that day, I attach a Post-it™ to my monitor to remind me.

Two types of To Do Lists are basic:

- Master To Do List
- Daily To Do List

A Master To Do List is a running list of things you need to do. You won't always have time to do something the instant you think of it. Nor do you have to. Write the thought down on a Master To Do List before you lose it. You may want to consider having two Master To Do Lists, one professional and one personal, rather than one long combined version.

Keep your lists simple. When you make up your Daily To Do List, refer to your Master Lists and your calendar for the actions you need to take. As you take action on an item, you can use symbols to show the status of your efforts:

WC = Will Call
CB = Call Back
LM = Left Message
NA = No Answer
X = Action Started

Finished? Cross it off.

Here's a time-tested Daily To Do List that really works. Give it a try. Think of what you did today. Most or all of your actions will fit into these five sections:

| CALL | DO |
|---|---|
| – BALDWIN INC. ABOUT SEMINAR<br>– MIKE ABOUT GALLEYS<br>– COPIER SERVICE FOR REPAIR | – DRAFT CH. 6 OF NOVEL<br>– CATCH UP ON FILING<br>– FINISH PROPOSAL FOR KAY ANDERSON<br>– UPDATE CREDITS LIST<br>– REWRITE DOBBS ARTICLE LEAD |

| SEND | MEET | ERRANDS |
|---|---|---|
| – MANUSCRIPT TO N.Y.<br>– THANK YOU TO MARY PINKERTON<br>– PROPOSAL TO ANDERSON | – AMY 2:00 P.M. ABOUT PROJECT<br>– GREG 4:30 P.M. TO DISCUSS ART CHANGES | – PHOTOCOPY ART AT PATRIOT'S<br>– BANK<br>– POST OFFICE<br>– BUY COPIER PAPER |

I'm always making lists of things to do. Then like Arnold Lobel's Toad, I spend the rest of the day searching for it and wondering what I am supposed to be doing.

Decide where you want to keep your Daily To Do List and put it there. Make it a habit. Put it in one section in your Planning Notebook or keep it in a pocket page at the front of the binder. One writer clips it to his calendar. Another puts her lists on clipboards. Some days she charges ahead doing things without referring to her list. But she says, "If I get immersed in something else, I know my clipboard will draw me back."

Remember to choose a place that fits your personality. The clipboard that works for one writer may turn into a drill sergeant for another.

## Managing Routine Information

Writers, like most people, lead busy lives. The more ways you can pare down routine tasks, the more time you'll save. Here are some quick files you can create on or near your desk that will help you speed up finding and sending information.

### ROLODEX®

Although many companies make desktop card files, Rolodex®, the principal manufacturer, has become a household term. The Rolodex® is an efficient unit for storing names, addresses, and information. The plastic or metal holders come in various sizes and usually have a 500- to 1,000-card capacity. Each unit comes with a supply of cards and one set of alphabetical guides. The cards are easy to remove and snap back into place after data is added. There's no worry about cards falling out or getting lost.

Divide the Rolodex® into color-coded categories tailored to your needs, just as you have your files. You may want to expand your Rolodex® beyond names and addresses. File the cards alphabetically within each category. You can put directions on how to get to specific places you visit infrequently. Some possible categories are listed on the next page.

- Yellow Pages/Services
- Business Contacts
- Work Associates
- Clients
- Organizations/Associations

- Travel
- Lending/Borrowing
- Birthday/Holiday List
- Location (where I put what)

Rolodex® also makes electronic organizers in both pocket and desktop models that can interface with some computers.

### QUICK-REFERENCE NOTEBOOK

You refer to some information often: charts, maps, area codes, schedules, lists, quick how-to instructions, and directions. Store such quick-reference information in plastic page protectors in a three-ring binder. Create a computer section in your Quick-Reference Notebook or, if it's handier, make a separate notebook and store it near your computer.

### QUICK-GRAB ORGANIZER

In a desktop organizer, keep a supply of frequently used forms and stationery, such as invoices, contracts, order forms, postcards, letterhead, memo forms. Remember the **O**ften-**O**ut, **S**eldom-**S**tashed formula? If you use these items **o**ften, keep them **o**ut in the open on your desktop.

### QUICK-READ TRAY

Everyone has materials that need to be read. Separate bulky from brief "to-be-read" items. Put magazines, manuals, and books you plan to read in a basket or shelf. Put materials you can skim—pamphlets, newsletters, periodicals, photocopied articles—in a letter tray. Tuck a highlighter pen into the tray. It's surprising how much reading you can get through if you're put on hold on the telephone or have a few spare minutes before a meeting. Traveling? Take a few Quick-Read items for commutes or airport waits. This habit really helps you stay current with your reading.

### MODEL CORRESPONDENCE NOTEBOOK

In a three-ring binder, store model letters you have composed. Refer to them when you need to write queries, proposals, thank yous, confirmation letters, marketing follow-ups. You can keep model letters on the computer, but it's convenient to scan hard copies of well-written generic paragraphs in a binder. Code each letter so you know where to find it on the computer.

Now, you have the tools you need to manage papers that require your immediate and ongoing attention. But how do you keep up with the flood when so much pours in each day? Even if you are all caught up, how *long* do you need to retain inactive papers? And how can you protect your papers in case of a disaster? Read on. In Chapter 6, you'll learn how to maintain your filing system once it's in place.

# CHAPTER 6
# Maintaining the System

## Seize the Day

Saul Bellow

**F**EW people dash right to their files and put away incoming papers. "I'll just pile this stuff here," they say. "Tomorrow I'll put it into my marvelous files."

Writers often have notorious drop-off points for incoming papers—on top of the watercooler, the edge of the desk, beside the copier. Despite periodic cleaning, the paper breeds, and the stacks grow higher.

No matter how many times I clear the deck, new papers pile up immediately. Within hours I'm back in a mess.

Murphy's Law applies exponentially to writers. "Paper multiplies in direct proportion to the number of horizontal surfaces available."

My writing piles fill whatever size desk I have. When I was little, I could obliterate my school desk. Now, my eight-footer has vanished!

There's more to life than filing. But it's difficult to find time to keep up with the flood of paper. You need a sensible plan for maintaining your filing system—a plan that helps you stay caught up without having to file every day.

*Carpe diem!* Seize the day with this Four-Step Maintenance Plan.

### Keeping Up with Current Filing: The Four-Step Maintenance Plan

#### STEP 1: CREATE A MASTER INDEX

Step 1 in keeping up with your current filing is to *create a Master Index*, either manually or by computer. Your Master Index serves as a handy one-stop tool that:

- Gives the big picture of your categories
- Helps you know where your folders are located
- Serves as a backup to your Paperdex™ in the drawer

Use a half-inch, three-ring binder to make a manual version of your Master Index. Here's what it holds:

- Areas/Categories List
- Category Code List
- Color Chart
- Sketch of File Locations
- Category Paperdexes™

Insert each of the first four items in plastic protector pages if you want.

### Areas/Categories List

You created this list, an overview of the categories you've established, in Step 3 of the Five-Step Organization Plan (see pages 18 and 19).

```
                    AREAS/CATEGORIES LIST


     MANUSCRIPTS AREA

     IDEAS
     PROJECTS  [for short writing projects]
     MOLLY ON THE OVERLAND TRAIL  [a longer writing project]
     DROPPED PROJECTS
     PAST PROJECTS


     MARKETING AREA

     MARKETING LEADS
     MARKETING ACTION
     CREDITS AND CLIPS


     FINANCIAL AREA

     INCOME
     EXPENSES
     MONTHLY TRANSACTIONS
     TAXES


     REFERENCE AREA

     WRITING MECHANICS REFERENCE
     WRITING SKILLS REFERENCE
     WRITING GENRES REFERENCE
     BUSINESS AND LEGAL REFERENCE
     MARKETING REFERENCE
     GENERAL REFERENCE


     ADMINISTRATIVE AREA

     FORMS
     WRITING BUSINESS  [your company name]
     GROUPS/ORGANIZATIONS  [one folder per group]
     WRITERS' ASSOC. OF AMERICA  [many folders if more involved]
     MASTERS
```

## Category Code List

To help you remember what your prefix codes stand for, make an alphabetical list of your category codes. Here is an example:

```
                    CATEGORY CODE LIST

    BL/R       BUSINESS/LEGAL REFERENCE
    CR         CREDITS AND CLIPS
    DPR        DROPPED PROJECTS
    EXP        EXPENSES
    FM         FORMS
    GRP        GROUPS/ORGANIZATIONS
    IDEA       IDEAS
    INC        INCOME
    MAS        MASTERS
    MKT/A      MARKETING/ACTION
    MKT/L      MARKETING/LEADS
    MKT/R      MARKETING/REFERENCE
    OT         MOLLY ON THE OVERLAND TRAIL  [Abbrev. project name]
    PPR        PAST PROJECTS
    PR         PROJECTS
    REF        GENERAL REFERENCE
    TAX        TAXES
    TRANS      MONTHLY TRANSACTIONS
    WAA        WRITERS' ASSOCIATION OF AMERICA
    WB         WRITING BUSINESS  [Abbrev. your company name]
    WG/R       WRITING GENRE/REFERENCE
    WM/R       WRITING MECHANICS/REFERENCE
    WS/R       WRITING SKILLS/REFERENCE
```

## Color Chart

You created this chart when you set up your categories (see page 45). It shows which colors have been used and which ones are available for any new categories.

| RED | YELLOW | BLUE | GREEN | PURPLE | ORANGE | PINK | BLACK | BROWN | GOLDENROD |
|-----|--------|------|-------|--------|--------|------|-------|-------|-----------|
| EXP | TRANS | TAX | INC | WM/R | WS/R | GRP | CR | MAS | BL/R |
| WB | IDEA | PR | MKT/L | | | WAA | REF | FM | |
| WG/R | | DPR | MKT/A | | | | | | |
| | | PPR | MKT/R | | | | | | |
| | | OT | | | | | | | |

## Sketch of File Locations

In Chapter 2, you sketched your workspace to help you inventory your files. Redraw this sketch, but leave out the location codes. Now jot down the category codes on the sketch to give you a bird's-eye view of where all of your categories live. Notice that the boxes in the corner have disappeared since the papers have either been filed or tossed.

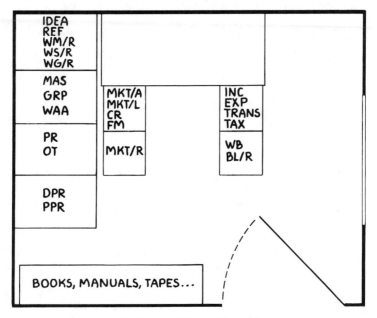

### Category Paperdexes™

Make photocopies of the Paperdexes™ for all of your categories. Three-hole-punch the pages and then arrange them alphabetically by their Prefix Codes.

Periodically update your Master Index as you add or delete subjects and cross-references. To update, either pencil in the changes or make new copies of the Paperdexes™. At first, update your Master Index often—every two or three months. After categories and subjects stabilize, once or twice a year should be sufficient.

You can use tab divider pages to separate the Master Index into sections. Label the spine of the binder "Master Index."

In an office setting, make as many copies of the Master Index as you need: one for your desk, one for home use, and copies for others, such as a secretary or colleague, who may need to use your files.

When a new secretary started in our department, her orientation time was incredibly fast. I gave her the Master Index and in less than ten minutes she understood our complete filing system. She could find papers in any of the files in our offices.

A word of caution: If you have too many copies of the Master Index floating about, it's harder to keep them all current.

You can also store a Master Index file on your computer. Here's how. Get all of your Paperdexes™ from the file drawers and alphabetize them. Then key the Paperdexes™ into one large computer file. For each Paperdex™ page, key in where the category is located in your workspace. As you create new categories, add them alphabetically by the code to your computerized master list. You can add other information to this computer directory later, such as your Workspace Inventory, Record Retention Schedule, and Disaster Recovery Plan.

### STEP 2: ESTABLISH AN INTERIM FILE

Step 2 in keeping up with your current filing is to *establish an Interim File*. It serves as a short-term parking spot for papers until you have time (or are in the mood) to file.

You say, "I already have this—the bottom drawer of my desk!" Ah, but that's the to-be-filed *pile*. That infamous stack is too formidable to tackle.

For me, maintenance is a bear. If I liked filing better, I wouldn't wait until papers piled up a mile high.

Some people keep a To Be Filed Folder directly behind the Paperdex™ in each category. This decentralized approach works fine if you don't mind walking to each location to prefile your papers.

The Interim File, on the other hand, is a central place to stash papers you need to file. Rather than having a mound of materials waiting to be filed, you presort your papers into separate hanging folders. This provides faster access to recently acquired information.

Include in an Interim File only those categories that aren't current or active, such as the **IDEAS** or **WRITING MECHANICS REFERENCE**.

Don't include in an Interim File categories that are critical to keep up-to-date, such as **INCOME** and **EXPENSES**. File incoming papers for those categories promptly.

You will need these supplies to set up an Interim File:

- Plastic file folder crate(s)
- Hanging file folders and plastic tabs

You can organize an Interim File by category or by area.

### By Category

Assign one filing *category* per hanging folder. Use the straight-line filing approach and arrange folders in alphabetical order according to the Prefix Code.

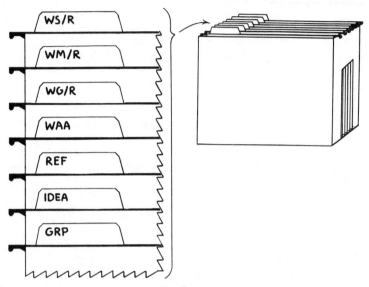

### By Area

Assign one filing *area* per hanging folder. Use the straight-line filing approach and arrange the folders in alphabetical order according to the area name. List on the tab which Prefix Codes are to be filed in that folder.

Choose the method that best suits you. Some writers prefer having a folder for each category, even if it means more folders.

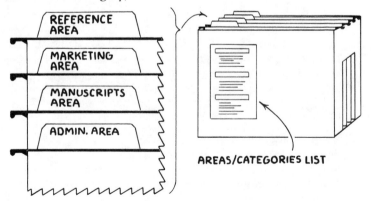

My Interim File has expanded to two plastic crates. I'd rather pre-sort my papers into categories right away. It saves me a step. Otherwise, when I file, I have to wade first through the papers from the broad area folders, and put them into categories, before I can decide the subjects.

Others prefer to sort by area. They're satisfied if the papers are at least in the right vicinity, until they are filed.

Keep your Interim File in a convenient location near your desk, but not necessarily on it. As new papers come in that can wait until later to be filed, put them in the appropriate folder in the Interim File.

Remember, the Interim File is *not* a permanent place to store papers! Clean it out periodically or it could become an annex to your existing files. Follow Steps 3 and 4 to learn how to file quickly papers temporarily stored in an Interim File.

## STEP 3: USE THE CODE-A-PILE APPROACH

Step 3 in keeping up with your current filing is to *code a pile of papers to be filed*. You streamline your filing time when you code a large batch of papers for a specific category in one sitting. (Just code, don't file yet.)

To Code-a-Pile you need:

- A folder from your Interim File
- The Master Index
- A pencil

Remove the papers from one folder in your Interim File. Find the Paperdex™ for your category in the Master Index and do this:

- Decide the subject for each item
- Look up the subject in the Paperdex™ to find its assigned code
- Print the code on the item in the upper right-hand corner
- Enter appropriate cross-references on the Paperdex™
- Set the item aside to be filed
- Repeat this process until you've coded all the items from the folder

If a subject isn't listed in the Paperdex™, decide whether to enter it as a new subject or to interfile the papers within another already-

**87**

established subject. (File folders for new entries are made during Step 4. Just print the newly assigned code on the item to be filed, and continue coding the rest of the papers in that interim folder.)

Don't lose momentum. Set problem papers aside and continue coding the rest of the pile. If deciding what to name a subject is difficult for you, ask a colleague who does similar writing. You can also get subject ideas from indexes of books related to your category.

Coding papers will soon become so routine that you'll not only code at your desk, but in such time-wasting places as waiting rooms, buses, and commuter vans.

You may not have time to file these coded papers right away. No problem. Return them to their interim folder. Since they are coded, you're one step closer to filing them.

Once papers are coded, move on to Step 4, speed-filing.

### STEP 4: USE THE SPEED-FILE APPROACH

Step 4 in keeping up with your current filing is to *put away coded papers*. You can file a large stack of papers faster if it's coded. It doesn't matter how much time has passed between Steps 3 and 4. The bonus is that different people can do the two steps—administrators, secretaries, project team members, or collaborators. They won't have to guess where you want the papers to go—the codes point the way.

Here's what you'll need:

- Coded papers from the folders in the Interim File
- Actual category (the drawer or box where the category is kept)
- Filing supplies (folders, labels, marking pens)

Here's what you do:

1. Take coded papers from one interim folder
2. Sort coded papers
3. File the coded papers in the categories, one letter or number at a time

If you entered a new subject in the Paperdex™ during the Code-a-Pile step, make a folder for it. (Be sure to check color and tab position before labeling the folder.)

### *The A–Z Method Categories*

Sort the papers by the *letter* in the code—all the As together, Bs next, and so on. Don't be concerned about the number in the code until you actually file.

### *The Prefix Method Categories*

Sort the papers in numerical order by the *number* in the code—all the -1s, then the -2s, and so on.

This Four-Step Maintenance Plan helps you keep up with filing and refiling. But file cabinets can hold only so much. Sooner or later the dam bursts. Walls don't automatically recede to make more space. The more nonessential stuff you keep, the less free space you have for what is important.

Beyond the financial costs of storage, someone ultimately has to clean out the archives, whether it's due to death, merger, moving, or flood. Read on to learn how, when, and why to prune your files.

## Weeding Out Unneeded Papers

How long should you hang onto drafts and manuscripts? That's a tough call. A century after Mark Twain's classic *Adventures of Huckleberry Finn* was published, a granddaughter of one of Twain's contemporaries discovered 665 pages of the original manuscript in a California attic. Twain's many additions and changes reveal strong insights into the creative process.

Some documents have clearly defined life spans. Other documents you can keep indefinitely—selected drafts, certain research notes, interview records, support documents. You decide how long you want to retain these. Laws vary from state to state. Contact a local attorney, accountant, and tax preparer for guidelines.

Create a written Record Retention Schedule. Whole books are written on this subject. This schedule allows you to replace sporadic pitching sprees with a time-dated plan. It controls how long papers live in your active and inactive files and when you dispose of them. If you work for a company, ask for a copy of the company and/or department Retention Schedule.

## Moving Inactive Records

As you learned earlier, papers are either pending or nonpending. The smaller your workspace, the more important it is to keep only pending or active files close at hand.

If you have a four-drawer filing cabinet, use the middle two drawers for your most active categories. Those drawers are the easiest to reach. File categories you use less often in the top and bottom drawers.

Transfer active records when they become inactive. Put them into storage boxes, which are less expensive and require less space than steel cabinets. Move the boxes away from your immediate work area—across the room or to the basement, storage closet, or records center.

Or transfer records at regular intervals, such as the end of the year, or during an "Operation Clean-Up" Week. At that designated time, also weed out unneeded documents. One company stages a contest called "In the Bin for Din." Those who transfer or toss the most papers win tickets to a dinner theater. Another company turns its file cleaning into a benefit for the community. For every pound of files the employees toss out, the company donates one pound of food to a local charity.

## Protecting Vital Documents

If you experienced a disaster tomorrow, how quickly could you get back into operation? Could you—from memory—list all your current deadlines and responsibilities? Do you know what books are on your shelves, what resource materials and documents are in your files, and what equipment is in your workspace?

Consider these true-to-life disasters: A novelist, whose home burned to the ground, lost his entire work in progress. A student's entire master's thesis disappeared because of a glitch on a rented computer. A self-publisher's electronic equipment vanished when his office was burgled—gone were his countless computer files.

Once everyone is accounted for after a disaster, the number one concern is getting back to business as soon as possible. The pieces don't automatically fall back in place after a calamity. Insurance helps in recovering material losses. But you should also develop a Disaster Recovery Plan for your writing business. Such a plan sets forth an orderly process for getting up and running again.

A step-by-step Disaster Recovery Plan does the following:

- Provides for safety
- Protects your papers and property
- Minimizes loss of work time
- Helps maintain financial stability
- Reduces exposure to liability

A catastrophic event can take many forms—tornado, fire, flood, equipment failure, power outage, vandalism, theft, even terrorism.

To be prepared, everyone should have basic emergency procedures in place—phone numbers, evacuation plan, food and water supplies, first-aid kit, fire extinguisher, water and gas shut-offs.

In creating your Disaster Recovery Plan, also consider these business-related questions:

- **What precautions do I need to take to safeguard my records?**
  Think about ways of protecting original manuscripts and important documents—safe-deposit boxes, backup disks or tapes, and off-site storage . . .
- **What vital records do I need to meet my critical obligations?**
  Think about urgent professional and financial commitments—invoices, current projects, and calendar items such as looming deadlines, assignments, contracts, and seminar materials . . .
- **What resources do I need to meet these obligations?** Think about workspace, equipment, materials, and funds—computer, telephone, desk, chair, and office supplies . . .
- **What paperwork do I need to stay in operation?** Think about ongoing responsibilities and long-term commitments—marketing, administrative, manuscript, and financial files . . .
- **What permanent records do I need to protect?** Think about ownership documents—copyrights, trademarks, current agreements, articles of incorporation, registration numbers and receipts for office equipment, policy numbers, and loan records . . .

Create your own Disaster Recovery Plan based on your answers. Keep one copy of the plan on hand in your **WRITING BUSINESS** category. Store an additional copy along with computer disk backups and vital papers away from your workspace, such as in a safe-deposit box, a neighbor's home, or a colleague's office. (Chapter 10 has more on disaster planning for your computer and documents and programs on your hard drive.)

What are the odds of your needing a Disaster Recovery Plan? Don't assume that a disaster can't happen to you. Is making a plan really worth your time and effort? Yes. Planning definitely pays.

With good risk management, you prepare for the worst and anticipate major problems. Preplanning, backups, and duplicate copies prevent hasty postdisaster decisions that you may regret later.

Many businesses, small and large, have learned firsthand the importance of having a Disaster Recovery Plan. One newsletter writer's computer was stolen. Because he had backup disks stored at a neighbor's home and complete records for his insurance, he was up to speed three days later. Another rescue occurred when a major Midwest bank went up in flames one Thanksgiving Day. Thanks to a detailed, well-rehearsed disaster plan, the bank arranged for temporary office quarters for 1,500 employees, and relocated critical backup records on just four hours' notice.

## Closing Up and Gearing Up at Year's End

Whether you operate on the calendar year or July 1st to June 30th, the close of the year is time to tie up loose ends and get ready for a fresh start. This is easier if you follow the Four-Step Maintenance Plan.

To make sure nothing is overlooked, create a Year-End Checklist. Modify your list to meet your needs and fit your schedule. Make it as detailed as you want. An example of a writer's checklist is shown below.

Begin working on the items on your Year-End Checklist in late fall—perhaps October, if it's a slow month.

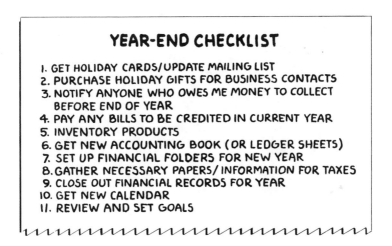

### YEAR-END CHECKLIST

1. GET HOLIDAY CARDS/UPDATE MAILING LIST
2. PURCHASE HOLIDAY GIFTS FOR BUSINESS CONTACTS
3. NOTIFY ANYONE WHO OWES ME MONEY TO COLLECT BEFORE END OF YEAR
4. PAY ANY BILLS TO BE CREDITED IN CURRENT YEAR
5. INVENTORY PRODUCTS
6. GET NEW ACCOUNTING BOOK ( OR LEDGER SHEETS)
7. SET UP FINANCIAL FOLDERS FOR NEW YEAR
8. GATHER NECESSARY PAPERS/ INFORMATION FOR TAXES
9. CLOSE OUT FINANCIAL RECORDS FOR YEAR
10. GET NEW CALENDAR
11. REVIEW AND SET GOALS

Your system is up and running and you know the basics of maintenance to keep it rolling. The next chapter tells how to move a writing project from the spark of an idea to a complete manuscript.

# CHAPTER 7
# Organizing Writing Projects—Start to Finish

## From Here to Eternity

James Jones

**W**HEN you first begin a writing project, especially if it's a major one, you may think you'll be working on it "from here to eternity." During that millennium, you can accumulate volumes of paper for the project.

*Gone with the Wind* probably started innocently enough—an idea and a few notes. By the time Margaret Mitchell finished the manuscript, who knows how many drafts she had, not to mention research notes, correspondence, and memos.

No matter what the length or type of project—whether it's a short story, grant, screenplay, article, novel, press packet, or manual—maintaining control is crucial to a well-oiled writing system.

I used to spread my work out on my office floor. Mid-project, I'd accidentally step on the papers or roll my chair across them. So I shifted the paperwork from the floor to my desk, where it now overflows to my computer printer stand and file cabinets.

Writing moves in stages. So does organizing manuscripts from start to finish. Here's how to set up files to store your ideas and manuscripts.

## Setting Up an Ideas Category

Whatever your genre, you're in the business of harvesting and storing ideas. They may be the kernels leading to a how-to article or a novel that makes readers reach for a Kleenex®.

Be ready for the creative flash. Keep a pad and pen in your briefcase, glove compartment, and nightstand so you don't lose that fleeting inspiration.

Sometimes words and scenes flow through me as if someone were dictating. But I'd better be writing them down, even if I'm in the dentist's waiting room. I often write in bed in the wee hours, even though the lines run together in the dark.

At a children's writers' conference, the prolific writing team of Audrey and Don Wood once described their brainstorming technique. They rummage through their four thousand–plus accumulation of ideas looking for something that "makes you laugh, something that makes you cry. There's a magic that happens. Ideas begin to combine in a web. It's incredibly moving."

The inexplicable does happen. Three unrelated ideas can meld together to form the core of a rollicking book. Try "dragon," "umbrella," and "marshmallow" and see what happens. You can't explain it—that's the beauty of writing. Wherever you go, be on the alert for ideas.

One of the writers in my critique group carries index cards in his pocket for scribbling ideas. I scrawl mine on bank deposit slips, envelopes, napkins, whatever's handy. I tend to remember them by the color of paper I've written them on.

While researching an article on caves in New Mexico for a nature magazine, I realized I could zero in on stalactites for another publication. I wrote myself a note on a paper bag to stash in my idea file.

What's the state of *your* idea cache? Chaotic or shipshape? If thrown together into one bulging folder or box, the squibs you've saved so diligently are like a circuit breaker on meltdown—a solid, useless lump. Separate your brainstorms, storing like ideas together under specific subject headings in an **IDEAS** category.

If you're a generalist, one category could house both nonfiction and fiction ideas. Some headings could be the same for either nonfiction or fiction:

| | |
|---|---|
| *Future Projects* | "Starter" material (general) |
| *Titles* | Catchy titles that could spark a whole project |
| *Words/Phrases* | New words and phrases; creative combinations |

Make the topics meaningful to you and your special interests. The prefix letters "IDEA," can represent the category name. The following is a sample nonfiction **IDEAS** Paperdex™.

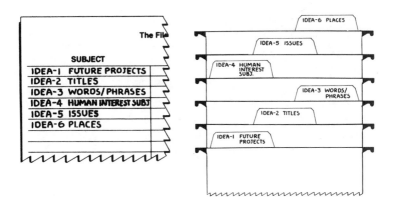

Here's a closer look at two of the subjects listed.

- **Human Interest Subjects.** If the lives of people like Maya Angelou, Jackie Joyner-Kersee, or Will Rogers intrigue you, store your ideas in *Human Interest Subjects*.

  I'm a nurse at a hospital, but I also enjoy writing. I'm fascinated by people whose lives touch others' lives in a meaningful way—like the physician who reattached a young man's arms after a farm accident.

- **Issues.** The *Issues* folder can include any topic that intrigues you—drug awareness, peace, retirement, water conservation, or smoking. If a single issue outgrows this folder, create a separate folder for the topic.

    I'm an ardent environmentalist. While hiking, I met some loggers in a mountainside camp and we talked at length. Later, I jotted down their worries, economic problems, and views, and stashed them in my ideas file. That conversation evolved into an in-depth documentary on logging versus the environment. The loggers' views added the balance of a different perspective.

Similarly, you can create a fiction **IDEAS** category based on the sample that follows.

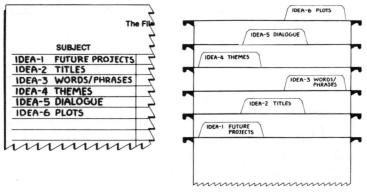

Here's a closer look at two of the subjects listed.

- **Themes.** Under the subject heading, *Themes*, file universal ideas that form the core of fiction writing: Life isn't fair, loneliness, self-control, laughter helps when the going's tough, unrequited love, and others.

    When I read *The Horn Book Magazine*, I highlight the themes noted in the children's book reviews. Then I jot them on a list and put it in my ideas file.

- **Dialogue.** Whenever you hear people gabbing or arguing, jot down the best phrases and file them under the subject *Dialogue*. Natural-sounding banter is the key to strong fiction writing.

I sat behind two elderly women on the bus and couldn't help overhearing their discussion about their doctors. I wrote it all down knowing I couldn't have made up such snappy give-and-take if I tried!

Your **IDEAS** category, nonfiction or fiction, works only if it's well thumbed. You have to *use* the ideas, not just *have* them. Make a date with yourself to cull through your file at regular intervals.

## Setting Up Writing Project Categories

Now, suppose your **IDEAS** category *has* sparked a nonfiction or fiction writing project. Whether it is short or long, you need a way to organize it and to understand the paperflow for your projects. The chart on page 102 shows an overview of where project papers live while you are working on them, where to move them when you're finished with them, and what happens to them if you drop the project.

Project papers generally fall into three groups:

| | |
|---|---|
| **ADMINISTRATIVE** | Nonmanuscript papers—memos, contracts, letters, FAXES, and phone messages |
| **WRITING** | Plans, outlines, drafts, and manuscripts |
| **RESEARCH** | Documents, articles, interview notes, photos/sketches, and maps |

### SETTING UP A SHORTER PROJECTS CATEGORY

You're working on several short writing projects—feature articles, people profiles, and a short story. Set up a category to house them called **PROJECTS**. Put the prefix code letters, "PR" and the working title on the folder tab. File these shorter projects alphabetically by the manuscript name.

A short project may require just one file folder for all related papers—administrative, writing, and research. But if the folder gets too bulky, use three manila folders, one each for administrative, writing, and research. Put all three into one hanging folder. To tell the three folders

# PAPERFLOW FOR SHORTER AND LONGER PROJECTS

| Shorter Projects | Longer Projects | Past Projects | Dropped Projects |
|---|---|---|---|
| • A current shorter manuscript lives in the PR category. | • A current longer manuscript lives in its own category near the PR category. | • A past project lives in the PPR category. | • A project you have temporarily or permanently dropped lives in the DPR category. |
| • When finished, a <u>copy</u> of the final version goes to MKT/A (Marketing Action, see ch 8). The manila folder, including the <u>original</u> version, goes to PPR, Past Projects. | • When finished, a <u>copy</u> of the final version goes to MKT/A (Marketing Action see ch 8). The rest of the category, including the <u>original</u> version, lives in its own section right behind PPR, Past Projects. | • Remove the manila folder(s) the project lived in while in PR (shorter projects) or in its own category (longer projects). Leave the hanging folder for another new shorter or longer project. | • Remove the manila folder(s) the project lived in while in PR (if it was a shorter project) or its own category (if longer). Leave the hanging folder for another new shorter or longer project. |
| • If dropped, it goes to DPR, Dropped Projects. | • If dropped, it goes to DPR, Dropped Projects | • Pencil a "P" for Past in the front of the code on the tab: PPR. | • Pencil a "D" for Dropped in front of the code on the tab: DPR. Arrange the folders alphabetically by title of manuscript. |
| | | | • House longer dropped projects behind the shorter dropped projects in DPR. |
| | | | • If you <u>reactivate</u> the project, erase the "D" and refile the folder in the PR category or in its own section near PR, if it's a longer manuscript. |

apart, add the letters "ADM," "WRI," and "RES," on the far right of the tab.

In the illustration below, the project "Burning the Candle in the Middle," requires three manila folders. The other shorter projects need only one folder each.

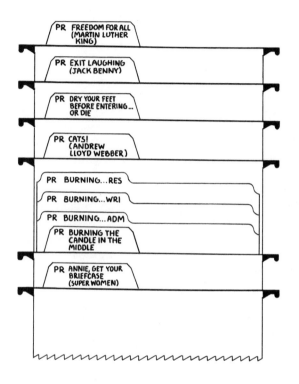

**SETTING UP CATEGORIES FOR LONGER PROJECTS**

You're working on a longer writing project, such as a book, a manual, or a curriculum guide. The project generates many papers—more than a single folder can hold.

Set up at least two separate categories to manage the project—**AD-MINISTRATIVE** and **WRITING**. If you have just a few research articles, put this information in one folder under the subject heading *Research* in your **WRITING** category. If your research is extensive, create a third category for that project, **RESEARCH**.

Follow three steps to set up these categories. After you've set up a file for one long manuscript, it will serve as a model for others.

Step 1   Choose appropriate prefix letters to represent the whole project. For instance, "LB" could stand for *Loon Book*, the working title for your project. To tell the three categories apart, add the letters "A," "W," or "R" to the code:
- LB/A for **ADMINISTRATIVE**
- LB/W for **WRITING**
- LB/R for **RESEARCH**

Step 2   Separate your project papers into the two or three categories you're using, decide on the subjects for each one, and create Paperdexes™.

Step 3   Using the code you've chosen, make corresponding file folders. This will keep the papers in your project separate and make refiling them easy.

Arrange the categories in the drawer. Some writers prefer putting the project's **RESEARCH** category first. Others store this at the back as an information tank for facts. You may prefer to put the project's **WRITING** category in front. Decide what will work best for you.

Here's how the categories for the LB project could look in the drawer and a closer look at each of the categories for the *Loon Book* project.

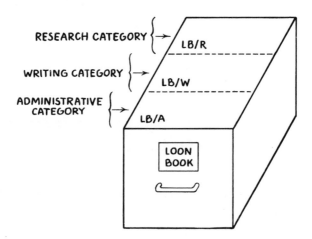

## ADMINISTRATIVE Category

The **ADMINISTRATIVE** category holds nonmanuscript papers related to the project.

Here is a sample Paperdex™ for the **ADMINISTRATIVE** category and descriptions of two subjects:

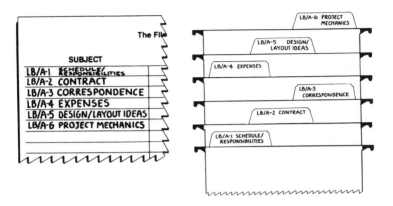

- **Schedule/Responsibilities.** How long do you have to complete your project? Two weeks? A month? A year? When you are working on a new project, establish deadlines, whether working on speculation or a go-ahead. You're more likely to stay on track with written time goals. Break the work up into manageable segments. File the due date and your goals for completion under the subject, *Schedule/Responsibilities.* If you collaborate, file in this folder a list of who is responsible for what.

- **Project Mechanics.** The subject *Project Mechanics* holds the editor's instructions, manuscript details, your style sheet for unusual conventions, and notes to yourself.

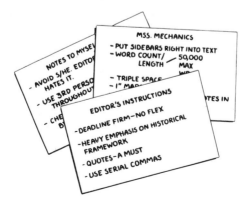

## WRITING Category

The second category, **WRITING**, houses all manuscript-related papers. You may want to separate your planning notes from your actual manuscript pages. Reserve a few folders at the beginning of the category for your prewriting preparations. Fiction planning could include idea/outline, setting, characters, plot, and details to check. For nonfiction planning, you could include idea/outline, permissions, art notes, and details.

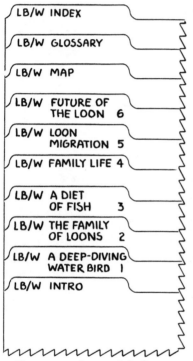

LB/W INDEX

LB/W GLOSSARY

LB/W MAP

LB/W FUTURE OF THE LOON   6

LB/W LOON MIGRATION   5

LB/W FAMILY LIFE   4

LB/W A DIET OF FISH   3

LB/W THE FAMILY OF LOONS   2

LB/W A DEEP-DIVING WATER BIRD   1

LB/W INTRO

Next in your **WRITING** category comes your actual manuscript. Include in each folder your rough drafts and final versions of each section or chapter. Some writers find it handy to put their latest draft in a three-ring binder while they're working on the project.

Give names to the chapters rather than referring to them as Chapter 1, Chapter 2, and so on. Chapter positions can change, especially in nonfiction. It's easier to keep track of the drafts when the chapter is called "A Diet of Fish" rather than "Old Chapter 4, New Chapter 3."

Use only code letters, such as *LB* for *Loon Book*. Do not use numbers. Arrange the folders in the same order in which the contents will appear in your final version.

If you use the straight-line approach, you can easily rearrange the folders if the chapter sequence changes. You can pencil in the current chapter number on the right side of the tab. It's easy to erase the number if the chapter order changes.

## RESEARCH Category

The optional third category, **RESEARCH**, includes the extensive background data you collect related to your writing project, such as photocopied articles, research notes, bibliographies, maps, interview notes, photos, sketches, and so on.

Here's a sample Paperdex™ for the *Loon Book* project and descriptions of two subjects:

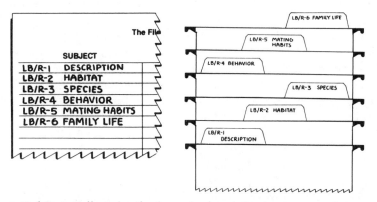

- **Habitat.** Collect details about the loon's environment and the region in which the bird lives. Gather specifics. Ferret out all details needed to bring the subject to life. This helps you avoid slip-ups. Some keen-eyed reader will know that the arctic loon's migratory path passes over California, but not over landlocked Kansas.
- **Species.** You should know everything about each species' life span—size, appearance, behavior, and family life. Include such details in the folder labeled *Species.*

  If the folder gets too full, or if you want information about only one species per folder, make additional folders using the same tab position and store them directly behind each other. Arrange these subtopics in alphabetical order. The folders may look like this:

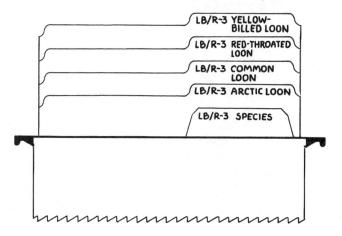

Keep a running list of your sources and code each one. For instance, make the first book you use *A*. (*Tip:* Indicate on the list where you found the book or source, such as "Carlsbad Public Library" or "from Priscilla Stevens.")

Then, as you take research notes, whether on cards, lined paper, typewriter, or computer, be sure to include your source code and date. For example, the source code for information from source *A*, page 48, would be A-48. Put the prefix code from your **RESEARCH** category in the upper right-hand corner of the research card and file it in the appropriate topic folder.

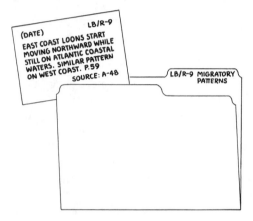

## Setting Up an Ongoing Project Category

Some writers deal with ongoing projects—newsletters, marketing letters, publicity, ad copy, or columns.

Columns, for instance, can cover an array of topics—politics, humor, book reviews, travel, foods/nutrition, computers, business, or health. If you have an ongoing column, set up a project file for that category. Call it, for example, the name of the column, the **SPORTS IN ACTION** category. When ideas, press releases, and information come to you for use in future columns, put them immediately into this category.

A columnist for a local paper set up a reference category right behind her project category. It houses background information on topics ranging from the Action for Elders Committee to the World Affairs Council.

# Tracking Your Writing Projects

Face reality. Some writers focus on one writing project at a time. But many juggle several assignments at once.

No sane person would have planned it this way, but both my book deadlines fell within the same two-week period. I'd work like crazy on Chapter 10 of one book, then switch gears and dog-paddle furiously on the other book. At night I'd edit in my sleep. The two texts began to blend together.

Balancing multiple writing jobs can be tricky. Questions like these come up:

- Which job takes priority?
- What are my deadlines?
- What did the editor say and when?
- What still needs to be done?
- What changes did I promise?

Three project management tools help you keep both the overview and the details of your current writing at your fingertips. (To purchase the Writer's Tool Kit, which includes these forms, use the order blank at the back of this book.)

| | |
|---|---|
| Projects Overview Form | Summarizes all your current writing projects |
| Project Status Form | Gives at-a-glance information on progress of each project |
| Ongoing Projects Log | Tracks successive projects or a project series for a single company |

### PROJECTS OVERVIEW FORM

Writers need to see the big picture. To summarize what's currently "on your writing plate," create a master record by using a Projects Overview Form. Store this form in your Planning Notebook, on a bulletin board, or on a clipboard, whatever suits you. The next page shows a sample Projects Overview Form.

| WORKING TITLE | DATE STARTED | NOTES |
|---|---|---|
| LOON BOOK | 1/4 | FIRST DRAFT DUE JULY 7 |
| CATS! (ANDREW LLOYD WEBBER) | 1/17 | PLAY'S "NINE LIVES" ARTICLE DUE BY MID-MAY |
| BURNING THE CANDLE IN THE MIDDLE | 5/7 | RESEARCH MANAGING JOB/HOME STRESS |
| EXIT LAUGHING | 5/21 | QUERY HUMOR MAGAZINES FOR REPRINT POSSIBILITIES |
| FREEDOM FOR ALL | 6/4 | VOTING RIGHTS RETROSPECTIVE DUE 6/15 FOR 7/4 PUB. |
| ANNIE, GET YOUR BRIEFCASE | 8/19 | FINDING THE ULTIMATE BRIEFCASE STYLE |

**PROJECTS OVERVIEW FORM** — **XXXX YEAR**

## PROJECT STATUS FORM

To know where you are on a *specific* writing project, use the Project Status Form. Regardless of the content and length of your work, this form gives at-a-glance information. As you work, track your progress by jotting on the form the date and what you did to move the job forward. Store the form with the manuscript. Here are two sample Project Status Forms—for short and long projects.

**SHORT PROJECTS STATUS FORM**

| PROJECT | DATE STARTED | DATE DUE | RESEARCH IDEAS | OUTLINE | FIRST ROUGH DRAFT | REVISIONS | FINE TUNING | FINAL | DATE SENT |
|---|---|---|---|---|---|---|---|---|---|
| CATS! (ANDREW LLOYD WEBBER) | 4/17 | 5/16 | 4/21 | 4/29 | 5/3 | 5/7 5/8 | 5/11 | 5/12 | 5/12 |
| BURNING THE CANDLE IN THE MIDDLE | 5/7 | | 6/30 | 7/10 | | | | | |
| EXIT LAUGHING | 5/21 | | | | | | | | |
| FREEDOM FOR ALL | 6/4 | 6/15 | 6/4 | 6/4 | 6/9 | 6/10 | 6/14 | 6/15 | 6/15 |
| ANNIE, GET YOUR BRIEFCASE | 7/8 | 9/30 | | | | | | | |

USE THIS FORM FOR SHORTER PROJECTS

| CHAPTER/ UNIT | OUTLINE/ FRAME | FIRST ROUGH | REVISIONS | FINE TUNING | FINAL | DATE SENT |
|---|---|---|---|---|---|---|
| CH. I DEEP DIVING BIRD | 1/15 | 2/3 | 2/6, 2/8 | 6/19 | 7/5 | 7/8 |
| CH. 2 FAMILY OF LOONS | 1/15 | 2/25 | 2/27, 2/29, 3/2 | 6/20 | 7/5 | 7/8 |
| CH. 3 DIET OF FISH | 1/15 | 3/15 | 3/21, 3/27 | 6/25 | 7/5 | 7/8 |
| CH. 4 FAMILY LIFE | 1/15 | 4/7 | 4/18, 4/22 | 6/28 | 7/6 | 7/8 |
| CH. 5 LOON MIGRATION | 1/15 | 4/28 | 5/2, 5/5 | 6/30 | 7/6 | 7/8 |
| CH. 6 FUTURE OF LOONS | 1/15 | 5/24 | 6/5, 6/10 | 7/2 | 7/6 | 7/8 |
| | | | | | | |
| | | | | | | |

**LOON BOOK** *TITLE*

USE THIS FORM FOR ONE LONG PROJECT

## ONGOING PROJECTS LOG

You may work regularly for one company, magazine, newspaper, or publishing house. If you do such writing, use an Ongoing Projects Log to track successive jobs. This form shows the dates and titles of your completed projects, such as articles, stories, books, manuals, annual reports, or publicity campaigns.

You can use the Ongoing Projects Log to track several different projects for a single company or use it to track a series of articles, perhaps a weekly column, for a newspaper. Here are two samples:

ONGOING PROJECTS LOG

COMPANY SPINNING CAROUSEL, INC.    CONTACT LUKE JOLLEY
ADDRESS 100 TENTH STREET    TELEPHONE (555) 546-2648
NEW YORK, NY 10010

| | DATE DUE | DATE SENT | DATE PUB. | COPY REC'D | DATE PAID | AMOUNT PAID |
|---|---|---|---|---|---|---|
| MATH CURRICULUM | 2/10/-- | 2/1/-- | 8/10/-- | 9/1/-- | 3/1/-- 9/1/-- | $1500. |
| GEOGRAPHY WORKBOOKS | 3/15/-- | 3/1/-- | 11/15/-- | 12/1/-- | 4/3/-- 1/10/-- | $2500. |
| READING STEP-AHEAD BOOKS | 10/1/-- | 9/15/-- | 7/1/-- | 7/15/-- | 10/15/-- 8/1/-- | $6000. |
| SCIENCE NATURE BOOKS | 10/15/-- | 9/30/-- | 8/1/-- | 8/31/-- | 11/10/-- 9/19/-- | $5000. |
| | | | | | | |
| | | | | | | |

ONGOING PROJECT LOG AS USED TO TRACK SEVERAL PROJECTS
FOR A SINGLE COMPANY

**ONGOING PROJECTS LOG**

COMPANY __THE WEEKLY PLANET__     CONTACT __VICTOR ANDREWS__

ADDRESS __1000 W. MAIN__     TELEPHONE __(555) 339-0000__

    __INKVILLE, NY 12345__

| | DATE DUE | DATE SENT | DATE PUB'D | COPY REC'D | DATE PAID | AMOUNT PAID |
|---|---|---|---|---|---|---|
| **"GETTING DOWN TO BUSINESS WITH ACCENT ON WRITING"** | 4/10/-- | 4/6/-- | 4/21/-- | 5/1/-- | 5/1/-- | $250 |
| **"LIFE ALONG THE RIVERFRONT"** | 5/10/-- | 5/6/-- | 5/22/-- | 6/1/-- | 6/1/-- | $250 |
| **"RED CROSS DIRECTOR UNFLAPPABLE AT HELM"** | 6/12/-- | 6/8/-- | 6/21/-- | 7/1/-- | 7/1/-- | $250 |
| **"BOOKBINDER'S PARADISE: RESTORING ANTIQUES** | 7/11/-- | 7/7/-- | 7/25/-- | 8/1/-- | 8/1/-- | $250 |

ONGOING PROJECTS LOG AS USED TO TRACK A SERIES OF ARTICLES
FOR A NEWSPAPER BY TITLE

## Dealing with Rough Drafts

Experts advise, "Write and rewrite." Ernest Hemingway rewrote the last page of *A Farewell to Arms* thirty-nine times. While you're fine-tuning your latest draft, how do you remember *which* draft you wrote *when*? You may accumulate five to twenty or more drafts of your manuscript! Files overflow with newer, tighter, and richer versions.

Which draft is most recent—the one labeled "Latest Revision" or one labeled "Fifth Revision"? Chronologically date your drafts. This prevents garbling the changes and doing extra work because the versions are mixed. Some writers add an extension number to the chapter name to signal the draft version. For example:

- FishDiet.01
- FishDiet.02
- FishDiet.03

The tough part is deciding when to discard your notes and drafts. Some writers cling to their old drafts like King Midas to his gold. Others are comfortable saving just pages three and fourteen from an old rough and tossing the rest. Still others automatically toss version number five after version number six is in hand.

Find your comfort zone for discarding drafts. Then write a discard date at the top with a fat marking pen. If you haven't referred to a previous draft within that period of time, you're probably safe tossing it. If you have recopied or typed the notes or narrative you first scrawled on yellow pads, it's safe to discard the originals.

## Dealing with Dropped Projects

You may occasionally drop a project, whatever your reason:

- A publisher kills it.
- You lose interest in it.
- Another project takes precedence.
- You can't find a buyer for it.

What do you do with the papers for a dropped project? Pencil the letter "D" for "Dropped" in front of the prefix letters "PR" on the folder so the code now reads DPR. File the folder in a separate category called **DROPPED PROJECTS**. Arrange the folders alphabetically by project title just as you have your active projects. Store in a nonpending area. If you reactivate the project, erase the "D" and refile the folder in the **PROJECTS** category.

DPR EXIT LAUGHING
(JACK BENNY)

## Restoring Order When Projects Are Completed

Your project is finished! You're elated to have the completed manuscript in hand. What happens to the project file folders? For some writers, closure comes naturally. Others add past project papers to a teetering heap on the shelf or stuff them into a box beneath the desk.

When I cross the last *t* on a project, my mind says, "There, you're done!" I shove the stuff into a drawer and in nanoseconds I'm thinking about starting or finishing another piece. It doesn't even occur to me that I need to do anything else with the project.

Before you move on to your next assignment, pare the files down while the project is fresh in your mind. Decide which papers are save-worthy. You may choose to keep parts of the manuscript for later use— scenes or major sections you had to cut. You might change the angle and write a new piece on the same topic. It can be worthwhile to keep your research and your outline. You may need them if an editor has a question.

Finally, move the svelte project files to your nonpending area. When a project is completed, add the letter "P" for "Past" to the beginning of the prefix code so it reads PPR. Then file the folder alphabetically in a **PAST PROJECTS** category stored in your nonpending area.

*Always* keep an original or a master copy of your final manuscript. Add a dated Post-it™ note marked "Final" to your master so you don't mistake it for a past version. Occasionally manuscripts get lost. You can avoid needless stress by keeping the master copy of the final version in your **PAST PROJECTS** category.

Remember the art of wastebasketry. Toss duplicate papers, scribbled reminders, and rough drafts crosshatched with lines and arrows. You don't need to keep a copyedited manuscript once it's published.

Voilà! You've set up your writing project files to house everything from the first sparks of inspiration to your final copies. And you have the tools to track them to completion.

But savvy marketing is the key to writing sales and success. Read Chapter 8 to learn how to manage your marketing efforts so you know what you sent where and when.

# CHAPTER 8
# Marketing Manuscripts

## Great Expectations

Charles Dickens

**A** WRITING truism says, "It won't sell from your desk drawer." Stellar as your manuscript may be, if it's languishing in a box under your bed or moldering at the back of your file cabinet, it's not going anywhere. If you have "great expectations" of finding a publisher, the broad area of *MARKETING* is for you.

This chapter shows you how to set up categories to organize any writing or writing-related services you plan to sell and how to use marketing forms to track your efforts. Targeting possible buyers is the first step in finding a publisher for your manuscript. Here's how.

## Targeting Buyers for Your Manuscripts

To sell your manuscripts, ask these basic questions:

- Who is my audience?
- Which publishers handle such material?
- Which markets shall I target?
- From past contacts, which editors might be interested in this piece?
- Who is my competition? What else is out there?
- When am I sending the manuscript and to whom?

Two filing categories and a handy marketing form will help you answer these questions easily.

*Categories*

**MARKETING LEADS**          Holds papers related to *your* potential markets

**MARKETING REFERENCE**      Holds papers related to *general* marketing tips

*Form*
Potential Markets Form    Lists possible markets for a specific
manuscript

## MARKETING LEADS Category

The **MARKETING LEADS** category houses contacts and leads specific to your future marketing. Any information you collect on potential markets lives in this category. Include all premarket plans: ideas for markets to tap, research into specific markets, and suggestions and brainstorms you have collected about possible ways to sell your work.

Your **MARKETING LEADS** category is unique to you because your leads are those you have personally sought out and developed—agents, publishing houses, and contacts at conferences. Set up the **MARKETING LEADS** category using the Prefix Alphabetic Method and the code MKT/L. Here's an example:

```
MKT/L  SERENDIPITY
       TIMES
MKT/L  PEPPERMILL
       PRESS
MKT/L  MARKET NEWS
MKT/L  GEORGIA AIR
       MAGAZINE
MKT/L  BOSTON
       COOPERATIVE
MKT/L  ARNOSKY,
       DON
```

I have a job because of a contact I made at a writers' conference. Instead of losing her business card (my usual style), I had put it in my Marketing Leads category. I was so excited to find it there when I needed it!

When you're ready to market your finished manuscript, you'll know right where to look for potential buyers.

## MARKETING REFERENCE Category

The **MARKETING REFERENCE** category houses general materials on marketing—tips, trends, and topical information.

**118**

I received some excellent information at a business seminar on a hot economic issue. Big deal. By the time I find it under my piles, the trends will be passé.

If you're just starting to write and don't have many reference articles on how to market, file them in one folder in your **MARKETING ACTION** category (described later in this chapter). If you have numerous articles on general marketing tips, set up a **MARKETING REFERENCE** category. Use the Prefix Method and the code MKT/R.

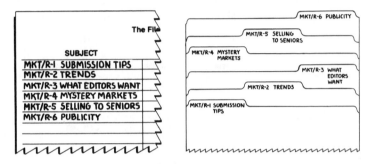

**POTENTIAL MARKETS FORM**

In this era of strong competition, focused submissions are doubly important. Editors detest receiving inappropriate manuscripts. Your careful research into potential markets will pay off.

A Potential Markets Form helps you to target markets for a specific project. Cull through your **MARKETING LEADS** and **MARKETING REFERENCE** categories for logical places to send your manuscript. Explore the possibilities listed in *Writer's Market*, newsletters, trade magazines, publishers' catalogs, and other resources. Spend time at a library or a comprehensive bookstore. Note which publishers carry material similar to what you've written. That way, you won't send satire to *Good Housekeeping* or nostalgia to *Omni*. Analyze a publisher's offerings by title, type, style, tone, and audience. Then record your findings on a Potential Markets Form. Use a separate form for each manuscript.

I generally do preliminary research for a nonfiction project and then send a query. That way I find out if there's a market for the project before I spend days or weeks writing it. But if it's fiction, I usually finish the piece before I seek a publisher.

**119**

Whether you do initial research or complete the manuscript before you query, hone in on potential markets before you send out your work. Fill in a Potential Markets Form with your premarketing ideas, listing good possibilities for places to sell a specific piece. Include the name and address of the publisher, editor's name, the source and page number where you found the lead, and any notes such as, "specializes in health-related info." or "buys photos, too." Staple the form to the inside of a left-tabbed manila folder. Label the tab "MKT/A *Name of Manuscript*," and file it in your **MARKETING ACTION** category. Below is a sample Potential Markets Form for a manuscript entitled "The World's Greatest Golf Courses."

Once you target potential buyers, you're ready to start marketing your manuscripts.

| POTENTIAL MARKETS FORM | | | THE WORLD'S GREATEST GOLF COURSES TITLE | |
|---|---|---|---|---|
| PUBLISHER/ADDRESS | EDITOR | SOURCE | NOTES/RIGHTS | DATE USED |
| GOLF WORLD | SIDNEY SMITHFIELD | MARKETING WEEKLY, MARCH 4, 19-- P.6 | 1ST NO. AMERICAN SERIAL RIGHTS | 5/19/-- |
| THE HIGHLANDER EDINBURGH, SCOTLAND | IAN McGREGOR | TIP FROM FRED CAMERON | 1ST BRITISH RIGHTS | 6/20/-- |
| RANCHO SANTA FE STAR | HILLARY MATTHEWS | SPORTS PAGE, SAN DIEGO GAZETTE, APR.11, 19-- | ONE-TIME RIGHTS | 7/22/-- |

## Submitting Manuscripts for Publication

Your submission package (whether a query, proposal with sample chapters, or a final copy) reflects your image. Make it professional.

Use black ink on white paper, no italics, no nine-pin dot-matrix printouts, no skimpy margins. Hand corrections signal, "I'm an amateur."

In this age of PCs and word processors, high-quality final copies are within most people's reach. Use your computer's spell-checker, proofread diligently, include headers and page numbers. Once your on-screen check is complete, pull a great copy from your printer.

If a submission is longer than five pages, editors prefer to receive it flat (unfolded) rather than in a number-ten business envelope. Never staple the pages. Use a large manila envelope, a padded envelope, or, for longer manuscripts, a box. Direct the manuscript to an individual or department, if the piece was done on an editor's go-ahead or on assignment. Print "REQUESTED MANUSCRIPT," "SPORTS DEPT.," "HU-MOR CONTEST," or other routing information in the lower left-hand corner of the package. For a professional look, use preprinted mailing labels.

When submitting your flawless final copy, your envelope should also include:

- A brief cover letter
- Pertinent credits and clips
- A self-addressed stamped envelope

### COVER LETTER

Keep your cover letter short. Two or three short paragraphs are plenty. Don't exceed one page. Refer to well-written letters from your past correspondence to make typing new letters fast. Keep sample letters in a Model Correspondence Notebook (see page 78). Or, store generic paragraphs about you and your work in your computer files. Pull up the paragraphs and build the letter around them, adding specific details to fit the piece you are submitting.

### CREDITS AND CLIPS

Pull a copy of your credits, resumé or curriculum vitae, and any appropriate clips of your published work from your **CREDITS AND CLIPS** category (described later in this chapter).

### SELF-ADDRESSED STAMPED ENVELOPE

Always send a self-addressed, stamped envelope (SASE) with your manuscript. Unless you include a manila envelope big enough to accommodate your clips and manuscript, a company doesn't have to return them. Affix the appropriate number of stamps, address the envelope to yourself, and fold it in half so it fits into the envelope you're sending. (Or get a slightly smaller manila envelope that can be mailed flat.) You'll find other submission tips in books such as *Writer's Market*, published yearly by Writer's Digest Books, 1507 Dana Avenue, Cincinnati, OH 45207.

# Tracking Your Marketing Efforts

Knowing what you've sent where and when is vital. Careful records can prevent duplication of effort and missed chances.

I sent off a query to an editor, got an okay on the proposal, and then couldn't find my copy or remember what I said I'd do!

The following category and three forms will help you stay on top of your marketing efforts:

*Category*
**MARKETING ACTION**  Holds papers related to your actual marketing efforts

*Forms*
Marketing Record Form  Lists your marketing efforts for a specific manuscript

Communication Log  Summarizes your contacts and communications concerning a specific manuscript or publisher

Marketing Overview Form  Gives you an at-a-glance view of all your current marketing efforts

## MARKETING ACTION Category

As the name suggests, the **MARKETING ACTION** category deals with your actual marketing efforts for specific manuscripts, queries, or proposals. As the chart on page 102 illustrates, the final version of your manuscript lives in the **MARKETING ACTION** category.

Everyone's **MARKETING ACTION** category is different. It may include free-lance writing, brochures, writing for a local newspaper, newsletters, bread-and-butter work, ghostwriting, work-for-hire, columns, a just-finished spy novel, curriculum writing, or contest entries. The size of your **MARKETING ACTION** category depends on how many writing projects you are selling at any one time. Some writers have only two or three folders in this category. Others have many folders. A glance at your category gives you a quick assessment of how much marketing you are doing. Again, if you have only a small amount of marketing reference information, such as trends, you can put it in a folder at the beginning of this category.

To set up your **MARKETING ACTION** category, use MKT/A for the code along with the manuscript title. Arrange folders alphabetically by title. Use a colored hanging folder with a corresponding colored plastic tab to serve as the category divider. Label the tab for this divider, MKT/A **MARKETING ACTION** and insert it in the center position.

If you submit many manuscripts to the same publisher, make the first folder in the category *Submissions to Publishing Houses*. Include in it running lists of what you have sent to each publishing house and when. You could use the Ongoing Projects Log described on page 111.

Use hanging folders with interior manila folders to house the projects you plan to market soon or are currently marketing. Label the plastic tabs of the hanging folders with the prefix code, MKT/A only and insert them in the left position. Use one left-tabbed manila folder per manuscript. Label the manila tabs with the code, MKT/A, and the name of the manuscript. File the folders alphabetically.

Although your writing topics may be unrelated, each folder in the **MARKETING ACTION** category contains similar information, including some marketing forms:

- Potential Markets Form
- Marketing Record Form
- Communication Log
- Cover letters
- Queries
- Proposals
- Go-aheads, on speculation or by contract

- Rejection slips
- Letters with suggestions
- Requests for changes
- Acceptances
- Correspondence
- Copyedited manuscript
- Galley/blue line
- Art notes

File the original or master copy of the completed manuscript in this marketing folder. Make several good copies if it isn't too bulky—a fifteen-hundred-word humor piece, for example. This ensures that you'll have a supply on hand during the marketing process.

As responses to your marketing efforts come in, file them chronologically in the folder, with the most recent responses to the back.

After you sell a manuscript, decide whether you plan to market it to another source. If so, leave the interior folder in the **MARKETING ACTION** category.

If not, remove the manila folder from the drawer and use the empty hanging folder for another manuscript you plan to sell. Add the letter "P" for past to the code on the manila folder you removed so it reads PMKT/A. That shows it's a Past Marketing Action folder. File it in your **PAST PROJECTS** category.

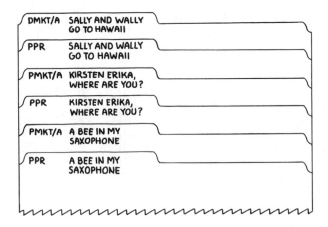

If you decide to drop your marketing efforts for the manuscript, print the letter "D" for dropped on the folder. Put the past and/or dropped marketing folder in the **PAST PROJECTS** category just behind the manuscript folder for the project. This keeps both the writing and the marketing papers for a project together. (Don't be concerned that the codes on the tabs don't match.)

The **MARKETING ACTION** category isn't limited just to selling manuscripts. You can create specialized sections, or even categories, that focus on your marketing efforts to promote your books, seminars, or consulting services.

## MARKETING RECORD FORM

A Marketing Record Form shows the steps you have taken in getting your manuscript published. Use a separate form for each query, proposal, or completed manuscript you send out.

Here's how to fill out this form:

1. Select a publishing house for your manuscript from the list on your Potential Markets Form. (On the form, note the date in the right-hand column, Date Used, to avoid sending materials to the same publisher twice.)
2. Write the manuscript title, date sent, publishing house, and editor's name on a Marketing Record Form.
3. Put a check mark in the Art column if you sent slides, photos, maps, or other graphics.
4. When your manuscript is returned or accepted, write the date received in the correct column, No or Yes.
5. If the response was No, select another publishing house from those listed on the Potential Markets Form. (Again, write the date in the Date Used column of the Potential Markets Form.)
6. When the manuscript is published, write in the date in the Date Published column.
7. Write the date in the Copy Received column when you receive a published copy.
8. Write the date paid in the Date Paid column and amount received in the Amount Paid column.
9. Add remarks in the Notes column, such as your rapport with the editor, any glitches in dealing with the publisher, encouraging rejection messages, and requests to rewrite and resubmit.

Here is a sample Marketing Record Form:

| DATE SENT | PUBLISHER | EDITOR | ART | NO/ DATE RET. | YES/ DATE ACCEPT. | DATE PUB. | COPY REC'D | DATE PAID | AMT. PAID | NOTES |
|---|---|---|---|---|---|---|---|---|---|---|
| 12/1/-- | AMERICAN EXECUTIVES | MARK WIGGINTON | PHOTO | 3/1/-- | | | | | | ED. THO'T TITLE WAS TOO CUTESY |
| 3/2/-- | THE CORPORATE WOMAN | RUTH JOHNSTON | PHOTO | | 5/2/-- | 7/1/-- | 7/7/-- | 7/7/-- | $1500. | RUTH NEW AT CW; EAGER FOR NEW WRITERS; EASY TO WORK WITH |

**MARKETING RECORD FORM**
TITLE **ANNIE, GET YOUR BRIEFCASE**

If you submit your work simultaneously to several publishers, you *must* indicate this in your cover letter. Entries in *Writer's Market* often indicate a publisher's attitude toward multiple submissions. Some find them acceptable, others tolerate them, and some loathe them!

## COMMUNICATION LOG

No writer can remember exactly every conversation with an editor, or verbal changes to each contract. Time plays tricks. It's easy to forget the sequence of events—calls made, letters received, notes written, or FAXES sent. Tracking what you said when, and what action you took when, is invaluable.

The way I remembered a discussion with my publicist was different from how she recalled the conversation. I had kept notes and realized she had mixed some facts and had completely forgotten others. The notes helped me to set things straight.

The Communication Log summarizes all communications between you and your publisher. Keep a separate log for each project. File it in the folder for that project in your **MARKETING ACTION** category. Each time you communicate with your publisher, note the following:

- Type of communication (C, F, L, or M—call/FAX/letter/meeting)
- Summary of the communication

- Follow-up to be completed
- Date follow-up is completed

The summary is not meant to be a verbatim record. Jot brief notes about what was said and done. If a telephone conversation is lengthy, key in your notes on the computer. Print them out and attach them to the Communication Log. (Delete the onscreen version.) Some argue that it's more efficient to store Communication Logs in the computer. But it makes more sense to keep all the marketing records for a project, including your Communication Logs, in one place—the **MARKETING ACTION** category. Here's a sample Communication Log:

```
                    COMMUNICATION LOG

NAME: MS RUTH JOHNSTON          POSITION/TITLE:  EDITOR
COMPANY: THE CORPORATE WOMAN    OFFICE HOURS:  M-F 8-4
ADDRESS:  40 W. FIFTH NY NY 10010    PHONE: (W) 593-5535 (H)
L=LETTER   C=CALL   F=FAX   M=MEETING    FAX: (555)591-5275
```

| DATE | TYPE | KEY POINTS | FOLLOW UP NEEDED | DONE |
|------|------|-----------|------------------|------|
| 8/15/-- | L | REC'D LETTER OF ACCEPTANCE FOR "ANNIE, | | |
| | | GET YOUR BRIEFCASE"; RUTH WOULD LIKE | SEND | 10/15/-- |
| | | MORE DETAIL ON WHERE TO BUY | REVISED | |
| | | BRIEFCASES; ALSO MORE PHOTOS; PIECE | COPY + | |
| | | WILL RUN IN MAR. | PHOTOS | |
| 11/10/-- | C | RUTH CALLED AND SAID PHOTOS WERE | | |
| | | GREAT + THAT THE PIECE WILL RUN IN | | |
| | | JAN. INSTEAD OF MARCH. | | |
| 3/25/-- | F | RUTH J. FAXED REQUEST FOR FOLLOW-UP | SEND | |
| | | ARTICLE TO RUN THIS FALL ON | OUTLINE | |
| | | RESOURCES FOR BUSINESS TRAVEL GEAR | | |

**MARKETING OVERVIEW FORM**

If you market numerous projects, a Marketing Overview Form gives you the big picture. (See example on next page.) It summarizes all of your current marketing efforts.

I record submissions on a big calendar and cross them off when returned. It's pretty simple because all I have to deal with is rejection slips. The whole system would self-destruct if I sold anything!

| MARKETING OVERVIEW FORM | YEAR __XXXX__ |
|---|---|
| **MANUSCRIPT TITLE** | **PUBLISHERS SENT TO** |
| CELIA OF THE MOUNTAINS | STRASSBERG HOUSE, MARSDEN & LLOYD, DOVER CLIFFS |
| PERSON TO PERSON: EMPOWERING VOLUNTEERS | COAST PUBLISHERS, INC. |
| SASSY TAKES A CHANCE | JACKSON, INC., SUNSHINE PRESS, YOUNG READER'S LIB. |
| COLUMNS: SPORTS HIGHLIGHTS FOCUS ON FRISBEES | KIDSPORT, INC. |
| A BEE IN MY SAXOPHONE | MUSIC DIGEST, ALL THAT JAZZ |
| SALLY AND WALLY GO TO HAWAII | PEPPERMILL PRESS |
| | |
| | |

## Tracking Your Credits and Clips

Keeping track of what writing has been published where and when is important. The term "credits" is used in two ways:

- Actual work—clipped (a "clip"), torn (a "tear sheet"), or photocopied
- Compiled list of your published work

Here are a category and two forms for keeping your credits up-to-date:

*Category*
**CREDITS AND CLIPS**    Holds listings of your published work along with clips and copies

*Forms*
Credits Summary    Summarizes your writing credits
Detailed Credits List    Cites all of your writing credits

### CREDITS AND CLIPS Category

Store copies of all your published work in a **CREDITS AND CLIPS** category. Be sure to add the name of the publication and the date on the first page of a clip if they don't appear. (Make a photocopy of newspaper articles—they yellow quickly, making them more difficult to copy later.)

Use hanging folders with interior manila folders in a straight-line arrangement. Label the plastic tabs of the hanging folders with the prefix code CR for **CREDITS AND CLIPS** and insert them in the left position. Reserve the first two folders for your Credits Summary and your Detailed Credits List (discussed below and on page 130). File the remaining folders alphabetically according to the name of the publisher or magazine, not an editor's name.

If you are new to writing, you may not have many credits yet. As you persevere, your **CREDITS AND CLIPS** category will grow from just a few pieces to a full drawer. Here is a sample **CREDITS AND CLIPS** category.

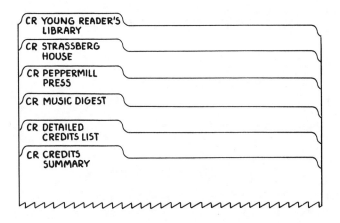

### CREDITS SUMMARY

If you have numerous credits, designate the first folder in your **CREDITS AND CLIPS** category as the home for your Credits Summary and the second folder for your Detailed Credits List. The Credits Summary provides an overview of your writing credits. Instead of listing the titles of ten interviews you've done for one magazine, say, "numerous interviews for (*magazine name*)." This summary often serves as a writer's resume.

Type a clean copy, then keep duplicates on hand. If you're publishing frequently, your Credits Summary can quickly become outdated, so don't print too many at one time. See the next page for an example.

**129**

Evelyn Hope Westin
5244 Penn Avenue North
Inkville, NY 12345

CREDITS SUMMARY

**Newspapers**
Journalist since xxxx. Numerous features for the *New York Sun Times* and its syndicates. Regular column, "Moving Forward," for *The Weekly Planet* since xxxx.

**Magazines/Encyclopedias**
Interviews for Business News, Redbook, Lear's, Working Woman, Cosmopolitan, and Life. Articles published in Reader's Digest and the New Yorker. Ten articles for National Geographic.

**Books/Scripts**
Voice of Peace: A biography of Martin Luther King, Jr. Presswood Press, Inc., xxxx; A Year With an Inner-city Teen, Webb House, Inc., xxxx; Poetry Behind Bars, Beeline Publishers, xxxx; City Halo, Beeline Publishers, in press.

**Teaching**
Writing seminars at the University of Minnesota since xxxx. Volunteer work teaching creative writing at Hudson Youth Reformatory since xxxx.

**Recognition/Membership**
The Alice J.R. Humphries Award for excellence in photojournalism, xxxx. Member, Writer's Association of America; President, Lake Region Writers' Association.

## DETAILED CREDITS LIST

For your own records, keep a Detailed Credits List that chronologically cites *every* piece you have published—its title, where it appeared, and the date. Include prizes or awards you receive for your writing, plus any published articles about you and your writing. Some writers group their credits by the type of writing.

If you need information on what you've published, your Detailed Credits List provides at-a-glance information. It's easy to keep this list current if you store it on your computer. Print hard copies as needed. See page 131 for two sample pages from one writer's Detailed Credits List.

Evelyn Hope Westin
5244 Penn Avenue North
Inkville, NY 12345

## DETAILED CREDITS LIST

### Newspapers

*New York Sun Times:*

"Sparking Reading in Tijuana's Poor: New Yorker teaches English to residents of Colonia Norte," 7/17/--.
"Somewhere Over Their Rainbow: Parents as one-on-one classroom volunteers," 7/24/--.
"This Fly Took Note of Appalachian Spring: A violinist's true tale," 9/5/--.
"Carl Rogers: A gentle giant seeking peace," 12/10/--.
"Regional Rejection Discards Trash Pact: Waste system goes back to drawing board," 11/17/--.
"Computer Graphics for the Information Age," 4/18/--.
"Math Science, and Beyond: Families learning science together," 5/2/--.
"Madison County's Covered Bridges," 6/1/--.
"I Spy: Spotting counterfeit money," 8/26/--.
"Lynn Johnston: Cartoonist breaking new ground," 6/7/--.

### National Geographic
"Sea Turtles: Making a comeback in the Cayman Islands," 4/--.
"Edinburgh: Mystical city out of the medieval past," 10/--.
"The Giant Crocodiles: Ambush on the Amazon," 11/--.
"Kauai: A tropical paradise's rebirth," 5/--.
"Australia's outback," 9/--.
"Grizzlies in Danger," 3/--.
"Laughing Whitefish Falls: Michigan's hidden secret on the Upper Peninsula," 10/--.
"American Patchwork: Quilting across the country," 1/--.
"Appalachia: America's front porch," 10/--.
"Whitney Classic: Cycling from desert to mountaintop," 8/--.
"Coyote Pass: Birthplace of a guitar," 11/--.

### Audio Tape Scripts for Serendipity Production, Inc.
"Remember the Alamo," 4/7/--.
"As You Like It," 7/5/--.
"Romeo & Juliet," 8/2/--.
"Lewis & Clark Chart a Course to the West," 8/26/--.
"Voyage to the Ends of the Earth: Christopher Columbus," 9/10/--.

**131**

# Dealing with Rejection

Sooner or later, most writers deal with rejection. Madeleine L'Engle had twenty-four rejections on her Newbery Award–winning *A Wrinkle in Time.* Another writer says, "I'm a known entity, so I get my rejections by phone." A third, with over one hundred books published, responded to her latest rejection slip by stomping on it.

The Marketing Record Form and Potential Markets Form help you handle rejections matter-of-factly. Use your Marketing Record Form to heighten your awareness as to why your manuscript was turned down.

Not all writers understand the strength of handwritten clues at the bottom of a form rejection or a personal letter. You may see only the "We are sorry" or the "We regret," not the statements that follow.

Notes one editor, "We never hear from half the writers to whom we respond. Considering how few we send personal notes to, this is remarkable."

Read the messages in a response letter carefully. Far from being casual addenda, these are strong statements. Write all comments in the Notes column on your Marketing Record Form. Learn from the suggestions and act: Revise, resubmit, or follow instructions. If you sense an implied second chance in a response letter, revise the manuscript and send it back, noting your action on the Marketing Record Form.

**MARKETING RECORD FORM**

TITLE CELIA OF THE MOUNTAINS

| DATE SENT | PUBLISHER | EDITOR | ART | NO/ DATE RET. | YES/ DATE ACCEPT. | DATE PUB. | COPY REC'D | DATE PAID | AMT. PAID | NOTES |
|---|---|---|---|---|---|---|---|---|---|---|
| 11/21/-- | STRASSBERG HOUSE | JAMES VAUGHN | LINE ART | 2/14/-- | | | | | | FOCUS MORE ON WILDERNESS ANGLE |
| 2/15/-- | MARSDEN & LLOYD | KAY KUECHEN | LINE ART | 5/14/-- | | | | | | REGIONAL APPEAL; TRY DOVER CLIFFS |
| 5/15/-- | DOVER CLIFFS | JULIE NOLL | LINE ART | | 6/10/-- | 3/1/-- | 4/10/-- | 7/15/-- 4/10/-- | $5000. | SHORTEN BY 600 WORDS + WE'LL LOOK AT IT AGAIN |

Some editors' comments do little to encourage. One writer received this five-word turndown: "I can't. I just can't." Other rejections, although brief, offer helpful advice. "We'll pass on this. Try again." Their encouragement is serious. Send something else right away and remind the editor of the request for more material.

Use your Potential Markets Form to put the 24-Hour Turn-Around Rule into action. Once a manuscript re-enters your door, it's out again within twenty-four hours. Here's how it works.

When you do get a rejection letter, your Potential Markets Form will answer the question "What next?" Just consult your list for another publishing house. Perhaps you've heard about a change in editors at one house or that a certain publisher is looking for manuscripts like yours. Make that your next choice. Type a new cover letter or query, and address a fresh envelope. Check your manuscript for smudges and wrinkles. Include a SASE (self-addressed stamped envelope), and put your manuscript in the mail.

Making a living as a writer wasn't always easy for the late Alex Haley, author of *Roots*. He said:

> For eight years, I wrote every day and would send out everything I could. I would get it back as quickly as the mail could bring it, with a little card that said, "Thank you for thinking of us."

Psychologically, fast action is important. Premarketing plans help ward off the old enemy, discouragement. When your manuscript zooms right back out of your office, you won't be trapped by the "It'll Never Sell" blues.

One word of advice: Don't toss your rejection notices if you're serious about the business of writing. They document your efforts for tax purposes.

When your marketing pays off and you sell an article or get a book contract, note your success on your Marketing Record Form. Since a contract is a legal record, file it with other business papers in your **WRITING BUSINESS** category.

Now that you know how to market your writing projects, you'll need to learn how to organize and keep track of another kind of paper—money! Chapter 9 shows you how.

# CHAPTER 9
# Tracking Financial Records

## The Burden of Proof

Scott Turow

**P**ICTURE an old-fashioned brass cash register, the kind that sat on a long wooden countertop in a general store. The till, as it was called, symbolized thriving enterprise. Each time the drawer opened, the bell rang, signaling how active the business was.

Your till doesn't have to be a sophisticated electronic cash box. A few folders may be all you need to house your financial papers. Whether you earn fifty dollars or fifty thousand dollars a year with your writing, the bottom line is still the same: It's the end of the month. Do you know where your finances are? The "burden of proof" rests with you.

## Understanding the Value of Keeping Clear Financial Records

Some writers wonder why they need to keep careful financial records.

I hate crunching figures. I much prefer developing an intriguing plot or researching the Taj Mahal. What fun is there in adding up a row of numbers I'll never look at again?

This chapter doesn't offer legal or accounting advice. Check with a competent professional if you have specific concerns. Here's what you need to know about your finances:

1. How much money do you have on hand?     (Cash on hand)
2. How much money do others owe you?    (Accounts receivable)
3. How much money do you owe others?    (Accounts payable)
4. How much money did you take in?     (Cash receipts)
5. How much money did you pay out?    (Cash disbursements)
6. How much money did you gain or lose?      (Profit/Loss)

There's no single right way to organize or maintain financial records, as long as you do these three things:

1. Keep records of your present financial condition.
2. Document *all* transactions.
3. Follow standard accounting principles.

You don't need to speak "accountantese" to understand the purposes of accounting. Simply put, accounting tracks the inflow and outflow of your money so you know what you owe, what you're owed, and what you own. That way, you track whether your finances are in the black or red. As the saying goes, "If your outgo exceeds your income, then your upkeep will be your downfall."

If you're in the business of writing, maintaining clear financial records is important, both for you and the IRS. Here's why.

1. **Records help you budget.** When you know where your writing income goes, you can adjust, cut back if needed, and make wiser purchase decisions.
2. **Records help you plan and project.** You'll have a sense of what works and what doesn't in your business. You can set short- and long-range marketing goals. You'll know when to eliminate unprofitable writing-related activities and whether to branch out into speaking, consulting, or other ventures.
3. **Records help you keep your credit rating healthy.** You stand a better chance of paying your bills on time when you know where to find them and whether you can cover them.
4. **Records help bolster your professional image.** Sending timely invoices for work completed shows that you're on top of business details. Good records help you trace late payments, royalty errors, and inaccurate billing.
5. **Records help you manage your inventory.** If you sell products such as books or tapes, you need to know how many units you've sold or given away as samples or review copies. When it's time to reorder, you'll know the number of units you'll need.
6. **Records save you time and money.** An up-to-date checkbook prevents overdrafts. You'll know not only where your checkbook *is*, but also how much money is in it! You can balance your statement faster and you won't run out of checks or deposit slips.

In order to maintain your financial records, the first thing you need to do is to set up your financial categories. Keep your writing finances separate from your personal finances.

## Setting Up Financial Categories

If you have few financial records, create one category called **FINAN-CIAL** with four subjects:

| | |
|---|---|
| *Income* | Cash Receivables |
| *Expenses* | Cash Disbursements |
| *Monthly Transactions* | Completed Income and Expense Records |
| *Taxes* | Tax-related Documents |

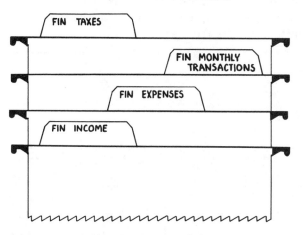

Otherwise, set up a *FINANCIAL* area with four categories to help you organize your paperwork: **INCOME, EXPENSES, MONTHLY TRANS-ACTIONS**, and **TAXES**.

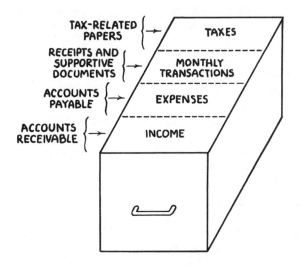

Subjects in each category will vary from writer to writer. Use those subjects that are relevant to your needs. Here are examples that work for many writers.

### INCOME Category

The **INCOME** category houses documents related to your business income. Arrange the subjects in whatever order you want.

Use the prefix code letters INC, and the color green for this category. (Think positively—think green!) Here's a sample index and how the folders might appear in the drawer:

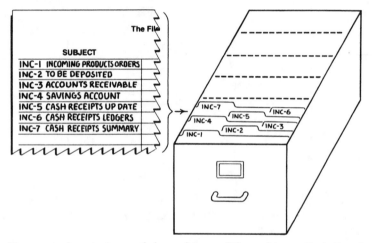

Here are descriptions of the subjects. (The subjects *Cash Receipts Ledger* and *Cash Receipts Summary* are discussed on pages 155 and 161.)

- **Incoming Product Orders.** Some writers sell written materials. If you receive direct-mail orders with attached checks, either process them immediately or put them in the Incoming Product Orders folder until you do. Since money is involved, the first folder in the **INCOME** category is a good place to stash checks and cash until you process the orders. Once processed, move the money to the *To Be Deposited* folder, INC-2.
- **To Be Deposited.** Unless you dutifully dash right to the bank the second a check or cash hits your hands, you need a place to store money until you have time to deposit it. In your *To Be Deposited* folder, keep incoming checks, a supply of checking account deposit slips, and your Cash Receipts Code List (see page 154).

- **Accounts Receivable.** Without careful records, income owed you can slip through the cracks. Use the *Accounts Receivable* folder, INC-3, to store any outstanding invoices. For every transaction, whether you sell a column, give a speech, or sell a book, prepare an invoice and put it in this folder. Then as checks come in, match them with their invoices.
- **Savings Account.** Keep your passbook in this folder, INC-4, along with recent bank statements for your savings account.
- **Cash Receipts Update Form.** For a current picture of how much money your business has, use a Cash Receipts Update Form similar to the one below. This form shows your total cash on hand and your accounts receivable (money owed to you). Design your own form and keep a supply in the **INCOME** category under the subject *Cash Receipts Update*, INC-5.

To know how much cash you have on hand, total your current checkbook balance, your savings balance, and any deposits you're going to make.

To this cash on hand, add the total of your accounts receivable, which is money owed to you for work completed. But remember, this is anticipated income, not actual income. To mix a metaphor, "the check is in the mail" is not the same as "hatched chickens."

Here is an example of a Cash Receipts Update Form:

```
                    CASH RECEIPTS UPDATE

                          As of _____
                               (Date)

          Source                        Amount
     Total current checking balance      $____


     Total to be deposited               ____


     Total savings account balance       ____


     TOTAL CASH ON HAND                   $____


     Total accounts receivable           ____


     TOTAL CASH RECEIPTS                  $____
```

The **EXPENSES** category houses documents related to your business expenses. Arrange the subjects in whatever order you want. You may decide to put subjects that need immediate or ongoing attention (bills or loan payments), toward the front of the file in an *Accounts Payable* folder. Use the prefix code letters EXP and the color red for this category. (Too many expenses? You'll be in the red!) Here's a sample index and how the folders might appear in the drawer:

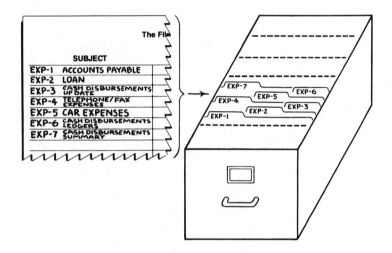

Here are descriptions of the subjects. (The subjects *Cash Disbursements Ledgers* and *Cash Disbursements Summary* are discussed on pages 159 and 161.)

- **Accounts Payable.** Accounts Payable is just a fancy way of saying bills. Keep unpaid bills and return envelopes in the *Accounts Payable* folder, EXP-1, until you pay them. If you pay for minor expenses with personal money, store the receipts in an envelope in this folder. When you accumulate enough to write a check, reimburse yourself.
- **Loan.** Your business may have a long-term loan, such as a car loan, or monthly payments on equipment, such as a copier. Designate one folder, for example EXP-2, specifically for loan-related papers rather than lumping them in with other bills in your *Accounts Payable* folder.

- **Cash Disbursements Update.** Just because you have a certain amount of cash on hand doesn't mean you can freely spend it. You need up-to-date figures to show what you owe so you can subtract that amount from your cash on hand. A Cash Disbursements Update Form helps you foresee what expenses you must meet with your cash receipts. It is not a budget. Create a worksheet like the one below. Your headings depend on your expenses. Use entries that apply to you. Print a supply of the forms you design and file them in the **EXPENSES** category under *Cash Disbursements Update,* EXP-3.

  Here is an example of a Cash Disbursements Update Form.

```
    CASH DISBURSEMENTS UPDATE FORM      For month of_____

         Expense                        Estimated Amount

    Speaking/teaching expenses                 $____

    Consulting expenses                        ____

    Product expenses                           ____

    Pay                                        ____

    Operating expenses

         Bank charges            ____

         Postage                 ____

         Shipping/handling       ____

         Meals/entertainment     ____

         Advertising             ____

         Office supplies         ____

         Copy service/copier     ____

         Computer expenses       ____

         Gas                     ____

         Parking                 ____

         Telephone/FAX           ____

         Gifts                   ____

         Professional services   ____

         Sales tax               ____

            Total                            ____

    Equipment expenses                         ____

    Professional development                   ____

    Loan payment                               ____

    TOTAL EXPENSES FOR MONTH                   $____
```

- **Telephone/FAX Expenses.** It's easier to trace specific calls when you house all telephone receipts and FAX transmission reports in one location, such as EXP-4.
- **Car Expenses.** If your business owns a car, keep track of repairs, oil changes, and other expenses by keeping all receipts in this folder, EXP-5. Mileage log books belong in the car. (As a safeguard, tear the log out month by month. If it's misplaced, you won't lose the whole record. Keep those pages in this folder.)

## MONTHLY TRANSACTIONS Category

The **MONTHLY TRANSACTIONS** category houses income and expense records once you complete transactions. A completed transaction occurs whenever someone pays you (inflow) or you pay someone (outflow). For every transaction you need written proof, such as:

- A paid store receipt
- A bank deposit slip
- A paid invoice or bill
- Your bank statement
- A canceled check

Transfer such papers from your **INCOME** and **EXPENSES** categories to your **MONTHLY TRANSACTIONS** category once you have finished your business.

Use the prefix code letters "TRANS" and the color yellow for this category. (Yellow is caution—remember, the burden of proof rests with you.)

For the **MONTHLY TRANSACTIONS** category, use four hanging folders, one for each quarter of the year. Label the plastic tabs with general headings so they don't need to be changed from year to year. Here's how a first-quarter TRANS tab will look:

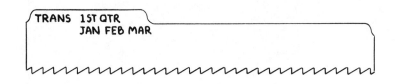

TRANS 1ST QTR
JAN FEB MAR

Use twelve manila folders, sequenced with left, center, and right tabs as shown. Label the tabs with a specific month and the year. File three manila folders in each hanging folder, one for each month, like this:

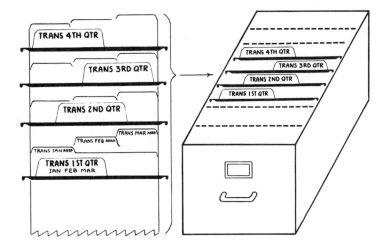

At the end of the year, take out the twelve manila folders and file them with past financial information. Make a new set of twelve manila folders for the upcoming year.

### TAXES Category

The **TAXES** category houses tax-related documents for your business for the current year. Use the prefix code letters "TAX," and the color blue for this category. (Do taxes give you the blues?) Your subjects will depend on how your writing business is set up: sole proprietorship, partnership, or corporation.

| | |
|---|---|
| *Sole proprietorship* | You are the sole owner. You keep all the profits, and are responsible for all loans, debts, claims, and complaints. |
| *Partnership* | You and your partner(s) co-own the business and share both the profits and losses. |

*Corporation*  Your corporation is a separate entity. It can own property, and earn, borrow, or owe money. Your personal assets can't be touched.

You may own a business in the form of a limited partnership, joint venture, cooperative, or franchise.

Here's a sample index for a **TAXES** category for a proprietorship and how the folders might appear in the drawer:

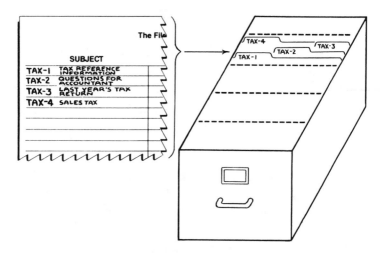

Here are descriptions of the subjects:

- **Tax Reference Information.** If you have general tax-related information from newspaper articles, brochures, or flyers, file them in a folder at the beginning of this category, TAX-1. Since tax laws change annually, be sure to weed out this folder every year.
- **Questions for Accountant.** Write down your financial questions and concerns as you think of them and file them in TAX-2. You'll have them all together for your next accounting meeting or call.
- **Last Year's Tax Return.** Keep the previous year's tax return handy for immediate reference, if needed, in folder TAX-3.
- **Sales Tax.** Writers with a product must pay sales tax. If you pay sales tax annually, one folder in your **TAXES** category is sufficient, for example, TAX-4. If you pay it monthly or quarterly, create a separate **SALES TAX** category and use the prefix code letters "STAX." It could look like the example on the next page.

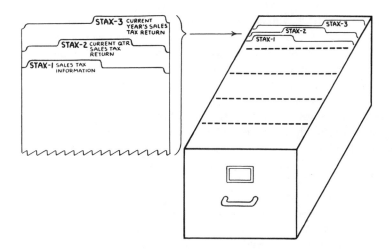

You've set up your categories. Now here's how to manage your paperwork for incoming cash.

## Managing Paperwork Related to Incoming Cash

Cash inflow occurs whenever someone owes you or pays you. Two kinds of forms will help you manage your inflow transactions:

Invoices
To show who owes you money, or from whom you received money, how much, and when

Bank deposit slips
To show how much money you put in the bank, from whom, and when

### INVOICES

When someone owes you money, document it with an invoice. Make sure you have a copy, whether it is paid immediately or weeks later.

I received a check with an attached note that said simply, "Thanks, Nate." There was no note of explanation. I didn't recognize the name. I didn't even have a record that somebody named Nate owed me money. It turned out the money was for some copy-editing I had done for a Nathaniel Allan several months before.

Not all buyers want an invoice. The publisher of your monthly column may send regular checks without requiring an invoice from you. Someone purchasing a copy of your book at a lecture you give may hand you cash and dash off. A client may pay you immediately for three hours of editing services and not want an invoice.

Buyers verify transactions with a canceled check. You, as the seller, need to document incoming transactions with an invoice, whether the buyer wants it or not. Create an invoice for your records. You'll be able to show whom you received the money from, for what, when you received it, and how it was paid—by cash or check (include check number).

You can create an invoice form on your computer, purchase a generic one at a stationery or office-supply store, or have a supply printed at a local print shop. A three-part form looks professional and is effective. Keep the pink copy for your records; send the white and yellow copies to your customer. The customer should return the yellow copy to you with the payment.

A completed invoice, like the example on the next page, should include this information:

1. Your name (or company name)/address/phone number
2. Date of billing
3. Company or individual being billed
4. Terms of payment and payment due date
5. Date product/service was delivered
6. Product/service being billed
7. Cost of product/service
8. Total amount due
9. Method of payment and "Paid" notation

What to do with an invoice when customer pays immediately:
• Give/send an invoice to the customer.
• File the pink copy of the invoice for your records with the payment (cash or check) in the *To Be Deposited* folder, in the **INCOME** category. The pink copy stays there until you deposit the payment in the bank.

What to do with an invoice when customer doesn't need a copy and plans to pay later:

- File the pink copy of the invoice for your records in the *Accounts Receivable* folder, in the **INCOME** category. It stays there until payment is received.
- If you don't receive payment by the agreed-upon date, send a copy of the invoice as a reminder.

What to do with an invoice when payment is received:

- Match the pink copy of the invoice in your *Accounts Receivable* folder against the yellow customer copy; then toss the yellow copy.
- If the check has an explanation attached, "payment for December issue article," tear it off on the perforated line and staple it to the pink copy.
- Mark the pink copy of the invoice "Paid," date it, and note the check number.
- File the paid invoice and payment (cash or check) in the *To Be Deposited* folder in the **INCOME** category. Both items stay there until you make your deposit.

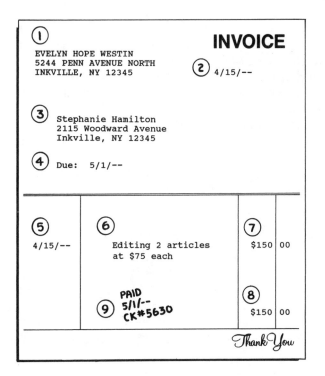

① EVELYN HOPE WESTIN
5244 PENN AVENUE NORTH
INKVILLE, NY 12345

**INVOICE**

② 4/15/--

③ Stephanie Hamilton
2115 Woodward Avenue
Inkville, NY 12345

④ Due: 5/1/--

| ⑤ 4/15/-- | ⑥ Editing 2 articles at $75 each | ⑦ $150 | 00 |
|---|---|---|---|
| | ⑨ PAID 5/11/-- CK#5630 | ⑧ $150 | 00 |

*Thank You*

## BANK DEPOSIT SLIPS

If you don't already have an account strictly for your writing business, establish a company name, and set up an account with your bank. (Your company name can simply be your own name.)

When you receive money, deposit it in your checking account first *before* you spend it. *Always* run *all* of your income through your business checking account so you have a record of money received.

If you need money for specific purposes, such as office supplies, withdraw it *after* it has been credited in the checking account. If you need only small amounts of cash, writing checks isn't practical. Pay the expense with personal money and have your business reimburse you. Don't be fooled into skipping these steps. Keep your records clean. It's critical.

I cashed a royalty check without depositing it first into my business account. A few months later, I'd forgotten completely that I'd received the payment. I called my publisher to ask where my check was. They told me I'd cashed it, but I had no record of it. Worse yet, I couldn't remember how I'd spent the money!

All checkbooks come with deposit slips or tickets. They are either included in the back of each packet of checks or are available in a booklet format. Request the type of deposit slip you prefer.

Keep a supply of deposit slips in the *To Be Deposited* folder. If the slips are attached in your checkbook, you may want to remove some and file them in this folder. They'll be handier to use if they're filed with the checks to be deposited.

When you fill out a deposit slip, *always* include the amount and the source of the money—the person's last name or company name. A deposit slip that lists only amounts is meaningless because it doesn't show where that money came from.

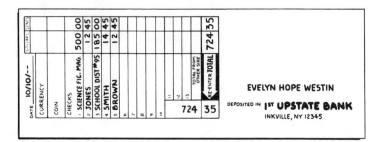

When you deposit the money, the bank keeps your deposit slip and gives you a receipt. But this generic bank form shows only the total amount deposited, not the breakdown you record on your deposit slip. Make a copy of your deposit slip before you go to the bank. Deposit booklets include carbon paper and two forms for each deposit—a white copy for the bank and a yellow copy for your records. Take both copies to the bank when you deposit your money. Ask the teller to validate both copies and return your copy to you. You don't need the bank's generic receipt.

When you return to your office, paper-clip all invoices related to that deposit to the deposit slip. *You should have invoices to corroborate all cash and/or checks you deposit.* File the deposit slip with attached pink invoices in the appropriate month's folder in the **MONTHLY TRANS-ACTIONS** category. You'll use them later to post your cash receipts, reconcile your bank statement, calculate your sales tax, and verify that month's income.

---

CRITICAL: *Always* enter in your checkbook the date and the amount of money you are depositing. If you forget to enter a deposit in your checkbook, it may seem like a windfall when you discover it. But until then, you won't know how much money you really have when you need it!

---

## Managing Paperwork Related to Outgoing Cash

Cash outflow occurs whenever you owe someone or pay someone. Two kinds of documents help you manage your cash outflow:

| | |
|---|---|
| Receipts or bills marked "Paid" | To show whom you owe and for what; what you paid and how much you paid |
| Canceled checks | To show you paid the bill |

### RECEIPTS OR BILLS MARKED "PAID"

The IRS wants you to verify every expenditure with a receipt. A valid receipt must include the following information: name of seller, date of sale, what was purchased, amount of sale, and check number.

A point worth repeating: If you pay for something with personal money, reimburse yourself with a business check and indicate that check number on the receipt(s).

If the expense is a meal, write on the back of the receipt with whom you had the meal and the purpose of the meeting. You must show that the meal was business related, not a social event.

File the receipts in the appropriate month's folder in the **MONTHLY TRANSACTIONS** category.

### CANCELED CHECKS

With the exception of automatic bank withdrawals, your canceled check is your proof that you paid a bill. If your bank doesn't return canceled checks and you need proof of payment, ask the bank to issue a copy of the check from its microfiche files. Your bank may charge a service fee for this. There may also be a limit as to how far back checks are kept by the bank.

File the current month's bank statement with the canceled checks in the appropriate month's folder in the **MONTHLY TRANSACTIONS** category. Keep your checks until the statute of limitations expires for an IRS or state audit.

A word of caution about voided checks. If you void a check, don't tear it up and toss it out. Mark it void and file it in the **MONTHLY TRANSACTION** category under the month in which you wrote the check. For good bookkeeping, you must account for all checks. When your bank statement arrives, put the voided check in the proper sequence with your canceled checks.

At the beginning of each month, reconcile your checkbook for the previous month. Instructions on the back of your statement will help you.

The two main reasons for reconciling your checkbook each month are to verify the accuracy of your check register and to make sure the bank hasn't made a mistake.

I didn't always keep track of my checking account. The bank does that, right? But then I started getting overdrafts and I learned that two deposits hadn't even been credited! I had made the deposits at an ATM [Automated Teller Machine], so I had no receipts. It took a month to straighten out the records. The ordeal cost me writing time and frustration. Now I pay closer attention to my checkbook.

Rarely, if ever, will the balance on the bank statement agree with the running balance you show on your check stubs or register. Some deposits may not yet be credited to your account, while other checks may not have cleared the bank.

I paid for some office supplies with an electronic check. I kept the transmission receipt, but forgot to record the amount I spent in my check register. I discovered my mistake when my bank statement arrived.

Reconciling your bank statement is the dénouement for all your checkbook mysteries.

## Tracking Your Income and Expenses

One way to answer the question "How much money did you take in?" is to add all your bank deposit slips.

And you could answer the question "How much money did you pay out?" by adding up the checks you wrote.

But these two figures give only totals. You need instant access to specific information: Where did the money come from and what did you spend it on? You must account for all the money you deposit and spend. The process of tallying this information, called posting, can be done either manually or by computer.

Computerized accounting is faster, more compact, and more accurate. It calculates, cross-checks the math, and recalculates instantly if you change entries.

### POSTING INCOME

Two tools will help you post your income:

| | |
|---|---|
| Cash Receipts Code List (CR Code List) | To classify your deposit sources |
| Cash Receipts Ledger (CR Ledger) | To track your income |

**153**

## Cash Receipts Code List

You can answer the question, "Where did the money come from?" by using a Cash Receipts Code List to classify your deposit sources. Tailor your Cash Receipts Code List to whatever ways you take money in—by writing articles, novels, grants, resumés, annual reports, by ghostwriting, editing, speaking, consulting, and/or other ways. Don't forget such non-writing sources as sales tax, shipping/handling, bank transfers, and loans. Include a last entry, Miscellaneous, for listings of deposits you're not sure how to classify. After you complete your list, assign a code number to each source.

Your Cash Receipts Code List may have only two or three codes, or be as diverse as this writer's list:

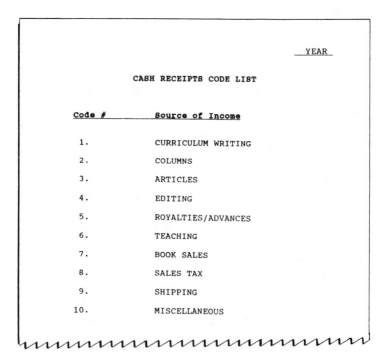

```
                                              _YEAR_


                    CASH RECEIPTS CODE LIST


        Code #          Source of Income

          1.            CURRICULUM WRITING

          2.            COLUMNS

          3.            ARTICLES

          4.            EDITING

          5.            ROYALTIES/ADVANCES

          6.            TEACHING

          7.            BOOK SALES

          8.            SALES TAX

          9.            SHIPPING

         10.            MISCELLANEOUS
```

Date your Cash Receipts Code List. Review it annually and make any necessary changes. Keep it in the *To Be Deposited* folder in your **IN-COME** category. Code each deposit slip when you make the deposit or just before you post it, as shown in the example on the next page.

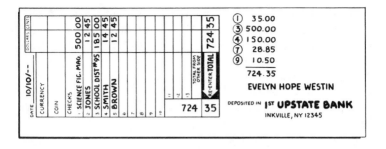

### Cash Receipts Ledger

You can answer the question, "How much money did I take in and when?" with a Cash Receipts Ledger. This financial record tracks your income. It shows at a glance how much money you deposited during the month and from whom you received it.

You can make your monthly ledger manually or by computer. To do your ledger manually, buy columnar sheets at an office-supply or stationery store. The sheets come in various formats or you can get a bound accounting book, such as the Dome® *Simplified Monthly Book-keeping Record* by Nicholas Picchione. To make your monthly ledger by computer, choose from many software spreadsheet programs.

Here is how to set up a Cash Receipts Ledger:

1. Label the first column, Date of Deposit.
2. Label the second column, Total of Deposit.
3. Label the remaining columns with the code numbers from your Cash Receipts Code List.

**CASH RECEIPTS LEDGER**

MONTH OF JAN, ~~XXXX~~

| DATE OF DEPOSIT | TOTAL OF DEPOSIT | (1) CURRIC. | (2) COLUMNS | (3) ARTICLES | (4) EDITING | (5) ROYAL./ADV. | (6) TCHG. | (7) BOOK SALES | (8) SALES TAX | (9) SHIP. | (10) MISC. |
|---|---|---|---|---|---|---|---|---|---|---|---|
| 1/7/-- | 50.00 | 50.00 | | | | | | | | | |
| 1/10/-- | 90.50 | | | | 75.00 | | | 10.00 | 2.50 | 3.00 | |
| 1/17/-- | 108.00 | | 75.00 | | | | | 30.00 | | 3.00 | |
| 1/24/-- | 300.00 | 200.00 | | 100.00 | | | | | | | |
| 1/31/-- | 140.50 | 50.00 | 75.00 | | | | | 10.00 | 2.50 | 3.00 | |
| | | | | | | | | | | | |
| TOTAL | 689,00 | 300.00 | 150.00 | 100.00 | 75.00 | | | 50.00 | 5.00 | 9.00 | |

The length of this ledger depends on the number of deposits you make each month. Because most small businesses generally make few deposits each month, their Cash Receipts Ledger isn't too long. The ledger width depends on how many deposit sources you use. Even if you have only one or two deposits, or your income from some sources is sporadic and small, use a Cash Receipts Ledger. The evidence adds up. At year's end, it's easy to see how much you have deposited in each classification.

Before you post your deposits, make sure that you have:
• Added the deposit slips correctly
• Entered the deposit amounts in the checkbook
• Filed invoices to corroborate each deposit
• Coded the deposit slip with the Cash Receipts codes

When you post deposits on your Cash Receipts Ledger, make sure you:
• Keep the Cash Receipts Code List handy for quick referral.
• Post all figures in black ink, except for totals, which can be in pencil.
• Enter the deposits from the coded deposit slips in chronological order.
• Check that the totals in the coded columns on each horizontal line equal the total deposit on that line.
• Check that the totals for all columns equal the total of all deposits for that month.

If you computerize your monthly ledgers, print a hard copy, double-check that all entries are correct, and file it in the *Cash Receipts Ledgers* folder in the **INCOME** category. If you do your monthly ledgers manually, you can store the columnar sheets in a binder, but it's less bulky to file them in the folder.

### POSTING EXPENSES

Two tools will help you post your expenses:

| | |
|---|---|
| Cash Disbursements Code List (CD Code List) | To classify your expenses |
| Cash Disbursements Ledger (CD Ledger) | To track your expenses |

## *Cash Disbursements Code List*

You can answer the question "What did I spend the money on?" by using a Cash Disbursements Code List to classify your expenses. Tailor your Cash Disbursements Code List to include whatever ways you spend money. You will probably have many more expense categories than income categories, but don't get carried away with the number of classifications. Make the last entry on this list Miscellaneous, for expenses you're not sure how to classify. After you complete your list, assign a code number to each type of expense.

Here's an example of one writer's Cash Disbursements Code List:

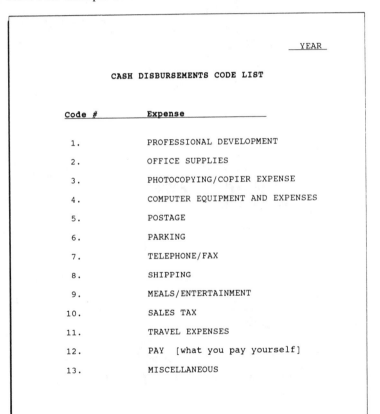

YEAR

CASH DISBURSEMENTS CODE LIST

Code #        Expense

1.        PROFESSIONAL DEVELOPMENT

2.        OFFICE SUPPLIES

3.        PHOTOCOPYING/COPIER EXPENSE

4.        COMPUTER EQUIPMENT AND EXPENSES

5.        POSTAGE

6.        PARKING

7.        TELEPHONE/FAX

8.        SHIPPING

9.        MEALS/ENTERTAINMENT

10.        SALES TAX

11.        TRAVEL EXPENSES

12.        PAY  [what you pay yourself]

13.        MISCELLANEOUS

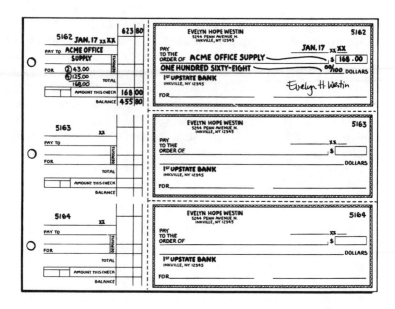

| CHECK NO. | DATE | DESCRIPTION | AMOUNT | √ | FEE | DEPOSIT/ CREDIT | BALANCE |
|---|---|---|---|---|---|---|---|
| | | | | | | | $ 623 80 |
| 5162 | 1/17 | ACME OFFICE SUPPLY | 168 00 | | | | 455 80 |
| | | ② 43.00 ④ 125.00 | | | | | |
| | | | | | | | |
| | | | | | | | |
| | | | | | | | |
| | | | | | | | |
| | | | | | | | |
| | | | | | | | |

EVELYN HOPE WESTIN
5244 PENN AVENUE N.
INKVILLE, NY 12345

**5162**

JAN. 17 xx XX

PAY TO THE ORDER OF **ACME OFFICE SUPPLY** ～ $ 168.00

ONE HUNDRED SIXTY-EIGHT ～ 00/100 DOLLARS

1ST UPSTATE BANK
INKVILLE, NY 12345

Evelyn H. Westin

MEMO

Date your Cash Disbursements Code List. Review it annually and make any necessary changes. Keep a copy of your Cash Disbursements Code List with your checkbook. When you write a check, jot the code number(s) for that expense on the checkbook stub or register. (See page 158.)

### Cash Disbursements Ledger

You can answer the question, "How much money did I pay out?" with your Cash Disbursements Ledger. This financial record tracks your expenses. It shows at a glance how much money you spent during the month and for what purposes.

As with the Cash Receipts Ledger, you can make a Cash Disbursements Ledger manually or by computer. Again, to do your ledger manually, buy columnar sheets at an office-supply or stationery store. The sheets come in various formats or you can buy a bound accounting book, such as the Dome® *Simplified Monthly Bookkeeping Record* by Nicholas Picchione. To make your monthly ledger by computer, choose from many software spreadsheet programs.

Here's how to set up a Cash Disbursements Ledger:

1. Label the first column, Date of Check.
2. Label the second column, Payee (to whom you write the check).
3. Label the third column, Check Number.
4. Label the fourth column, Check Amount.
5. Label the remaining columns with the code numbers from your Cash Disbursements Code List.

CASH DISBURSEMENTS LEDGER — MONTH OF JAN., ****

| Date of Check | Payee | Check Number | Check Amount | ① Prop. Devel. | ② Office Supp. | ③ Photo Copy/Copier | ④ Computer | ⑤ Postage | ⑥ Parking | ⑦ Telephone Fax | ⑧ Ship. | ⑨ Meals/Enter. | ⑩ Sales Tax | ⑪ Travel Exp. | ⑫ Pay | ⑬ Misc. |
|---|---|---|---|---|---|---|---|---|---|---|---|---|---|---|---|---|
| 1/12/-- | LAKE REGION WRITERS ASSOC. | 5160 | 20.00 | 20.00 | | | | | | | | | | | | |
| 1/15/-- | U.S.P.O. | 5161 | 8.00 | | | | | 5.00 | | | 3.00 | | | | | |
| 1/17/-- | ACME OFFICE | 5162 | 168.00 | | 43.00 | | 125.00 | | | | | | | | | |
| 1/17/-- | U.S.P.O. | 5163 | 10.00 | | | | | 5.00 | | | | 5.00 | | | | |
| 1/19/-- | US WEST | 5164 | 50.00 | | | | | | | 50.00 | | | | | | |
| 1/20/-- | COMMISSIONER OF REVENUE | 5165 | 20.00 | | | | | | | | | | 20.00 | | | |
| 1/21/-- | FANCY FIXINS RESTAURANT | 5166 | 12.00 | | | | | | | | | 12.00 | | | | |
| 1/27/-- | INSTY PRINTY | 5167 | 9.00 | | | 9.00 | | | | | | | | | | |
| 1/31/-- | E.H. WESTIN | 5168 | 300.00 | | | | | | | | | | | | 300.00 | |

The length of this ledger depends on the number of checks you write each month. The width depends on the number of codes you use. Even if you write only a few checks, use a Cash Disbursements Ledger. At year's end it's easy to see how much you have spent in each classification. If you use the computer, a hard copy of even a fairly extensive ledger will be only a few pages long.

Before you post your expenses, make sure that you have:
• Put all the required data on the check stub: date; to whom; for what; Cash Disbursements Code)
• Filed receipts to corroborate each expense

When you post expenses on your Cash Disbursements Ledger make sure you:
• Keep the Cash Disbursements Code List handy for quick referral.
• Post all figures in black ink, except for totals, which can be in pencil.
• Enter one check at a time in numerical order in the third column.
• Put the expense amount in the appropriate coded column(s). (See breakdown of Check #5162 on page 158.)
• Check that the totals in the coded columns on each horizontal line equal the total amount of the check on that line.
• Check that the totals for all columns equal the total of all the checks written for that month.

If you computerize your monthly ledger, print a hard copy, double-check that the entries are correct, and file it in the *Cash Disbursements Ledgers* folder in the **EXPENSES** category. If you do your monthly ledger manually, you can store the columnar sheets in a binder, but it's less bulky to file them in the folder.

### SUMMARIZING YOUR LEDGERS

You may be saying, "Enough! I've transacted, reconciled, and posted. All I want to know is how much money I made or didn't make!"
Pause. Take a deep breath.
To know exactly where you are financially at a given time, you can use these tools:

| | |
|---|---|
| Cash Receipts Summary | To provide an overview of the year's income |
| Cash Disbursements Summary | To provide an overview of the year's expenses |

With these summaries, you can see the entire year's figures at a glance and make comparisons without having to flip through twelve separate cash receipts ledgers and twelve separate cash disbursement ledgers. You can pinpoint problems and make projections.

Here's how to set up a Cash Receipts Summary:
1. List the deposit sources and their code numbers in the left-hand column.
2. Label the second column, Total, so your final figures are next to their sources.
3. Fill in the months across the top of the page.

Use your Cash Receipts Ledger to enter the monthly figures on this summary. Keep your Cash Receipts Summary in your **INCOME** category. Here is an example of one writer's Cash Receipts Summary:

| CASH RECEIPTS SUMMARY | | | | |
|---|---|---|---|---|
| | Total | Jan | Feb | Mar |
| 1. Editing | 225.00 | 75.00 | 75.00 | 75.00 |
| 2. Columns | 450.00 | 150.00 | 150.00 | 150.00 |
| 3. Articles | 300.00 | 100.00 | 100.00 | 100.00 |
| 4. Curriculum | 500.00 | 300.00 | | 200.00 |
| 5. Royalties/Advances | 2000.00 | | | 2000.00 |
| 6. Teaching | 450.00 | | 450.00 | |
| 7. Book Sales | 125.00 | 50.00 | 50.00 | 25.00 |
| 8. Sales Tax | 15.00 | 5.00 | 5.00 | 5.00 |
| 9. Shipping | 27.00 | 9.00 | 9.00 | 9.00 |
| 10. Miscellaneous | 18.00 | | 18.00 | |
| TOTAL | 4110.00 | 689.00 | 857.00 | 2564.00 |

Here's how to set up a Cash Disbursements Summary:
1. List the expenses and their code numbers in the left-hand column.
2. Label the first column, Total, so your final figures are next to their expenses.
3. Fill in the months across the top of the page.

Use your Cash Disbursements Ledger to enter in the monthly figures on this summary. Keep your Cash Disbursements Summary in your

**EXPENSES** category. Here is an example of one writer's Cash Disbursements Summary:

| CASH DISBURSEMENTS SUMMARY | | | | |
|---|---|---|---|---|
| | Total | Jan | Feb | Mar |
| 1. Professional Development | 230.00 | 20.00 | 200.00 | 10.00 |
| 2. Office Supplies | 73.00 | 29.00 | 32.00 | 12.00 |
| 3. Meals/Entertainment | 47.00 | 12.00 | 15.00 | 20.00 |
| 4. Copies/Copier | 49.00 | 9.00 | 18.00 | 22.00 |
| 5. Computer | 125.00 | 125.00 | | |
| 6. Postage | 34.00 | 10.00 | 16.00 | 8.00 |
| 7. Parking | 38.00 | 10.00 | 15.00 | 13.00 |
| 8. Telephone/FAX | 105.00 | 50.00 | 25.00 | 30.00 |
| 9. Shipping | 25.00 | 8.00 | 7.00 | 10.00 |
| 10. Sales Tax | 20.00 | 20.00 | | |
| 11. Travel | | | | |
| 12. Pay | 1950.00 | 300.00 | 450.00 | 1200.00 |
| 13. Miscellaneous | 178.00 | 59.00 | 54.00 | 65.00 |
| TOTAL | 2874.00 | 652.00 | 832.00 | 1390.00 |

## Managing Tax-Related Paperwork

Do you toss your W-2 or 1099 in a drawer in January and hunt for it on April 14? As the tax deadline approaches, some writers have long since received and spent or invested their refunds. Other writers postpone until the eleventh hour the chore of collecting records for filing their income tax return. With your financial records in order, doing your taxes will be less traumatic.

Five common questions sum up the basics about tax-related paperwork:

1. What tax-related records do you need to keep?
2. Where should you keep your tax-related papers?
3. What expenses can you deduct?
4. What happens if you're audited?
5. How long do you need to retain your tax-related records?

Remember, the information in this chapter is not legal or accounting advice. Check with a competent professional if you have specific concerns.

## WHAT TAX-RELATED RECORDS DO YOU NEED TO KEEP?

Tax-related papers include all records that support the financial side of your business. These can include:

- Bank statements
- Interest statements
- Canceled checks
- Ledgers
- Receipts
- Invoices
- Inventory records
- Calendar/appointment book
- Mileage logs
- Previous years' tax returns
- Contracts
- Correspondence
- Rejection notices
- Payroll books
- Wage/withdrawal reports

One tax adviser counsels:

> Your best protection is a well-kept appointment book. If you note on your calendar on January 14th—"12:30 lunch with Rainbow Press editor to discuss novel," it backs up your receipt for the $20.38 lunch on that day.

Don't forget to keep accurate records when you travel. The "envelope" approach works very well for on-the-road record-keeping. Before your trip, withdraw a reasonable amount of cash from your business account to use as travel money. (Use traveler's checks.) As you spend it, jot the date, purpose, and amount on the front of a number-ten envelope and put the receipt inside. At the trip's end, you'll have a complete record of your expenditures and the documents to prove it.

Then "balance" your travel money. The total of your receipts plus the unspent money should equal the amount you withdrew from the bank. Redeposit any unspent money in the bank. (Don't pocket the difference. You need to account for all money withdrawn from your business account.)

If you don't have time to deal with the envelope contents right away and you have money to redeposit, put the envelope in the *To Be Deposited* folder in your **INCOME** category. If no money is left, file the receipts in the appropriate month's folder in your **MONTHLY TRANSACTIONS** category.

## WHERE SHOULD YOU KEEP YOUR TAX-RELATED PAPERS?

To prepare your taxes you'll use information you have stored in your financial categories—**INCOME, EXPENSES, MONTHLY TRANSACTIONS**, and **TAXES**. (If you have few records, you'll have one category, **FINANCIAL**, with four folders.)

## WHAT EXPENSES CAN YOU DEDUCT?

What you can and cannot deduct as a writer changes frequently. Two magazines, *Writer's Digest* and *The Writer*, run tax-related articles early in the year. Save those tips and give them to your accountant.

Laws continually change, but certain basic deductions exist for writers.

You might struggle for some time before making any money and incur expenses long before you sell a piece. Your manuscript could sell for $1,000, but you might spend $700 on research expenses. At present, if you don't earn any money during a given year, you cannot deduct your writing expenses. But if you have even a small amount of income, you can claim expenses.

The way the law currently reads, you may declare a tax loss for three out of five years. But if you can document your writing efforts, the IRS may allow you to continue to declare the loss for subsequent years. Good records document that your writing business is a vocation, not an avocation.

For several years in a row, my writing income was less than impressive. The IRS auditor questioned my deductions, implying that my writing was a hobby. I whipped out a folder of rejection notices, my Potential Markets Form, and a sheaf of manuscripts. She dropped the matter.

A word of caution about independent contractors. The IRS particularly targets small businesses that classify workers as independent contractors rather than as employees. If you hire people to type, do mailings, assemble or ship product, or do other tasks, understand the IRS rules. If an independent contractor is reclassified as an employee, you are liable for tax penalties and interest on payroll tax assessments. The IRS bases its decision on whether a person is an independent contractor on twenty established criteria. Request a copy of this list from the IRS.

If you want to claim a home office deduction, check state and federal guidelines. To qualify, your home office must be used exclusively on a regular basis as the principal place of business. It needs to be the "focal point" of your business activity. Also, bear in mind that you can't take a home office deduction and declare a tax loss in the same year.

## WHAT HAPPENS IF YOU'RE AUDITED?

For starters, you don't want to be audited. Audits are stressful and time-consuming. Unfortunately, you don't have much choice in the matter. The IRS audits about one out of every one hundred returns chosen either at random or through a screening process. Take heart. Rarely will your entire return be checked and IRS policy says you won't be audited for the same reason two years in a row (if there is no change in your return after the first audit).

Often the examination is handled entirely by mail. If the audit is through a personal interview, you and the IRS examiner may negotiate a time and place most convenient for both of you. You are entitled to have a lawyer, CPA, or someone who has passed an IRS exam represent you at the audit. Even though it will cost you for this service, it's a good idea. A third party isn't emotionally attached to defending why you bought so many books or took six business trips to New York City in a contested year.

If you are chosen for an audit, the IRS isn't suggesting you are dishonest. The main reason for an audit is to verify the correctness of your reported income, exemptions, and deductions. But the burden of proof still rests with you, the taxpayer, not the IRS. If you can't identify the source of income, say a check for $500, the IRS assumes it's business income. If you can't document a deduction, it's disallowed. Even if you can support your claims with written proof, the IRS may still not allow the deductions, but your chances improve with good documentation.

If you don't have the necessary records at the time of the audit, you may take the records to a follow-up session. Ask what documents are needed or what other records will be adequate. You may appeal if you don't agree with the examiner's findings. See the IRS publications that explain taxpayer rights.

What's important is to be honest. You can't fabricate expenses or fail to claim income. If you do, you dig yourself into a hole you can't climb out of. Keep accurate financial records. And organize them so you can find them if you are audited. Don't run the risk one writer took:

A screenwriter friend received an IRS audit notice in his mailbox. At first he was panic-stricken, then enraged. He crammed every paper he could get his hands on into some grocery bags, marched downtown, and plopped them on the auditor's desk. He said, "The IRS wants receipts? They've got 'em!" He had a nitpicking session with an irritated auditor. My friend lost valuable writing time and legitimate deductions.

**165**

## HOW LONG DO YOU NEED TO RETAIN YOUR RECORDS?

How long you must keep records varies from state to state. One accountant counsels her clients to keep documents "preferably forever." But, generally, you need to keep records for only three years to cover the statute of limitations. If you fail to report 25 percent of your gross income, the limitation is six years. Technically, the IRS can check your returns back to Year One if you have failed to file or if you have filed a fraudulent return. Keep copies of your 1040s indefinitely.

Remember the six financial questions at the beginning of this chapter? Now that you're familiar with the categories and forms for managing your financial records, here's what you'll use to find the answers.

| *The question . . .* | *The answer may be found . . .* |
|---|---|
| How much money do you have on hand? | . . . on your Cash Receipts Update Form in your **INCOME** category |
| How much money do others owe you? | . . . in *Accounts Receivable* in your **INCOME** category |
| How much money do you owe others? | . . . in *Accounts Payable* in your **EXPENSES** category |
| How much money did you take in? | . . . on your Cash Receipts Ledger in your **INCOME** category |
| How much money did you pay out? | . . . on your Cash Disbursements Ledger in your **EXPENSE** category |
| How much money did you gain/lose? | . . . on your Cash Receipts Summary or Cash Disbursements Summary in your **INCOME** and **EXPENSE** categories |

You can manage your financial records manually or by computer. If you are considering purchasing a computer, upgrading your present system, or want ideas on how to organize your computer files, the next chapter will help you to make sound, long-term decisions.

**166**

# CHAPTER 10
# Bringing Computers into the System

Brave New World

Aldous Huxley

**T**HERE it stood—a symbol of emancipation. The gleaming electric typewriter that would be the ticket to instant manuscripts. No more hacking away on a clunky manual machine. What a sweet word: automatic.

After plugging in the ultraquiet Zephyr, it didn't take long to realize that the words didn't write themselves.

Today, when someone says, "I can't wait to get a computer—I'll be so organized!" it's like high-tech déja vu.

Scanners. CD ROMS. Virtual reality. It's a "brave new world."

A computer *is* invaluable. It speeds up writing and editing, transmitting information, and storing and finding records. But having a computer doesn't guarantee you won't "pile" the data in it. The same habits that cause disorder in your life B.C. (Before Computers) can transfer into your electronic world. You put information into the system and you:

- Forget what you named a file and spend your time searching for it.
- Misplace a file you started and create another with a similar name.
- Forget a file exists (along with three dozen others that should have been deleted ages ago).

You can adapt much of the File . . . Don't Pile!® System to organize your computer files just as you have the papers in your file cabinets. If you already have a computer and are eager to start organizing the information on it, go directly to the section called "Naming Computer Files" (see page 177).

If you haven't yet bought a computer, or if you plan to upgrade, here are some suggestions for organizing your purchase considerations.

## Buying or Upgrading a Computer System

Whether you're a first-time buyer or are preparing to upgrade your current system, you need to decide what you want your computer to do. Then do your research. As you gather information, you can file it in one pocket of your Action Notebook or in a desktop organizer. Or, if you have a lot of literature, create a temporary category called **COMPUTER PURCHASE**. Keep it with other Back Burner Pending categories in a drawer in or near your desk.

Computer systems range in price from modest to very expensive. It's essential to plan before you buy. After you define your software needs, take the advice of this expert:

> Find the software you need to accomplish your goals. Then buy the hardware to support that software. Be conservative—you'll rarely need all the bells and whistles offered.

Systems usually have their own terminology, although some terms are universal. IBM systems use directories, subdirectories, files. Mac systems use folders and files.

With the icon philosophy (using pictorial symbols to direct the user), terminology has become less system-specific. (See the next page for basic computer terms used in this chapter.)

### MAKING SOFTWARE DECISIONS

Here are some tips to consider before you buy your software:

- **Try many different programs.** Choices include word processing, databases (to organize information, sort, and alphabetize), file managers, spreadsheets (to handle inventory, accounting), and others. If you often need detailed resource material, you can buy software volumes such as encyclopedias, quotations, and almanacs. It's better to buy this software on compact disks so you don't tie up your hard drive with mounds of data. You'll need a CD ROM player designed for computer use to run them. CDs provide much more information for the dollar because of their large storage capacity and fast search capabilities.
- **Get key features with your word-processing software.** As a writer, a word-processing program will probably be your prime focus. If you work for a company, you must use whatever system is

## Computer Terminology

| | |
|---|---|
| *Software* | Programs, applications, and information that tell the computer how to work. Software is available on disks, CD ROM libraries, networks, and from other sources. |
| *Hardware* | Equipment used to run your software such as the computer, hard drive, keyboard, monitor, mouse, printer, and modem. |
| *Hard Drive* | Hardware that stores your software and files. |
| *CD ROM* | Compact disk read-only memory. Software can be read from a CD ROM but you can't store your own data on it. These disks can hold large quantities of data and information. |
| *Word-Processing Program* | Software that lets you type, edit, reformat, and rearrange text. |
| *Floppy Disks* | A flexible, removable disk for storing and retrieving data. Disks can vary in size, and some are encased in rigid plastic for protection. |
| *Hard Copy* | A printed copy of your computer data. |

in place. But for your own writing needs, decide what features are most important to you. Look for:

- Spell check
- Blocking
- Search and replace
- Grammar check
- Date code
- Macros
- Thesaurus
- Outline
- Indexing

Do you want the ability to change letter size and font? Create tables of contents? Indices? Graphs? Charts? View several screens simultaneously? Be sure you can easily change page numbering, headers and footers, and margins.

- **Talk with other writers.** Ask other writers what software they use. What do they love or loathe about it? Learn from others' purchasing mistakes.

  The graphics are terrific, but I can't make them mesh with my text.

  I wish the program were more user-friendly. You need a Ph.D. to run it!

- **Thumb through the manuals.** Compare the program manuals with reference books written by second-party users. The latter are often more practical. They're written in English (not computerese) and highlight special techniques with clear illustrations.

### MAKING HARDWARE DECISIONS

With computer technology moving forward at lightning speed, carefully chosen minor upgrades can enhance your present system. If you have extra money to spend, go for reliability rather than fancy extra features.

Here are some tips to consider before you buy your computer hardware:

- **Decide on your budget.** Include all the peripherals you may need—printer, mouse, modem, and so on.
- **Try different systems.** Work with different machines and software to find which meet the applications you need. Check with friends, colleagues, dealers, computer specialists, consumer guides, and reviews in newspapers and magazines.
- **Find out what equipment your software requires.** Investigate features such as the size of memory, number and size of disk drives, monitor size and screen color, whether a mouse is optional or required, external or internal.
- **Evaluate your computer's compatibility.** If you network with other writers or with publishing houses, computer compatibility is important.
- **Know whether you'll need a modem and/or FAX card.** Consider speed and whether the modem will be built-in or external. A FAX card is useful for receiving typeset proofs complete with graphics. When used in combination with a scanner, you can also send graphics.

- **Aim for a high-quality printer.** The way your words appear on the page reflects your professionalism.
- **Shop around—prices and services vary.** See below for additional consumer suggestions.

---

### Consumer Tips

- **Examine the warranty.** Know both what's covered and the quality of customer service.
- **Get referrals.** Check with others who have purchased from the dealer you're considering.
- **Know your repair options.** Expect ongoing maintenance repairs. Find out who will do repairs and where, whether in the shop or in your office. Understand fees, such as the minimum service charge and hourly repair rate.
- **Know your total costs.** Include such expenses as cables for peripherals (printers, scanners, FAXES).

---

The four basic hardware components you need to consider when you buy are: computer, keyboard, monitor, and printer. (Most systems also require a mouse.)

### *Computer*

The computer is a box that contains the central processing unit (CPU), memory, interface cards, hard drives, floppy drives, and CD ROM.

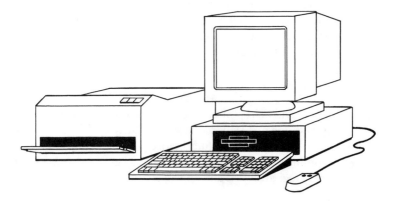

### Keyboard

Some keyboards, such as those with a laptop or notebook styles, are part of the computer unit. Others are separate. You'll spot extra keys, possibly some with unfamiliar codes or symbols. Try several keyboards to know what's comfortable for you. Response time, touch, pad size, even the sound, all vary. Check the resistance of the keys as you type— some are designed to spring back. You should be able to type with a light touch.

### Monitor

You view your work on a monitor screen. Some monitors are part of the computer unit; others are separate. Screen size and readability vary. Scrutinize on-screen material before you buy. It should be easy to read.

I have a monitor that rotates. It's perfect for creating the charts I need to insert in my reports. I can compare the documents vertically or horizontally and view partial pages side by side.

You can get color or monochrome (black and white, amber, or green).

### Printer

Printers vary in quality. Possibilities include dot-matrix, ink-jet, and laser. Choose tractor feed and/or friction feed, hand-feed, or automatic sheet feed. Ask for samples of the weight paper you can use.

Make sure the print is easy to read. A twenty-four pin dot-matrix printer produces almost letter-quality work. The high-quality laser printer produces camera-ready copy that can go straight to an offset printing press. The ink-jet is a good compromise—it offers good quality and speed, but is less expensive than a laser printer.

### Mouse

The mouse is a hand-held pointing device that moves the cursor left to right and up and down. A stationary track ball may replace the mouse. Try mouse-driven programs carefully before you buy. For writers accustomed to lightning-quick keystrokes, leaving the keyboard to work with the mouse may feel awkward and slow.

### *Modem*

A modem connects a computer to a phone. The system sends and receives information over telephone lines. Many publishers and editorial and production staffs (especially newspapers) receive manuscripts by modem.

You can use your modem to download work directly into a company's system, eliminating retyping and decreasing costs and errors. The computer can automatically send data on weekends or at night when you'll save money with the lower phone rates.

With a modem, you can connect with on-line data services or university database systems. Services are wide-ranging: networking with other writers, buying products, doing research, making travel reservations, and more.

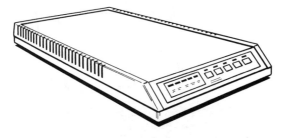

### *Scanner*

A scanner "reads" typed text, then downloads it into your computer. Accuracy, size, level of skill required, and costs vary widely. "It's the handiest clipper going," says one happy free-lancer. Battery-powered portable scanners are available for library and other research. (You must have a laptop to do this.)

## *Laptop Computers*

A laptop is a small portable computer with most of the benefits of a desktop computer. You can download the information from a laptop right into your main computer system or print directly from the portable. Laptops are handy for writing as you travel, for taking notes in interviews, for doing research away from your office, or for writing letters while on vacation or at conventions. Purchase considerations include:

- Weight
- Portability
- Readability of screen
- Size of screen
- Memory capacity

- Battery—work and recharge time
- AC power capability
- Compatibility with your desktop computer

## Learning How to Use a Computer System

Software is a tool. You don't need to understand the intricacies of *how* it does what it does. You just need to know how to use it.

Until the commands and procedures become automatic to you, use aids such as a keyboard template. Create a personal instruction guide— either in one section of your Quick Reference Notebook or as a separate binder. Note reminders about such basics as how to initialize or format disks, make back-ups, and create macros. Keep a running list of computer questions to ask computer-literate friends or take to meetings of your local software group.

Whether you store your data on a hard drive or a floppy disk, the directories or folders for your computer data are much like the Paperdexes™ for the categories in your office filing cabinets. The directories or folders guide you to the information you need.

## Naming Computer Files

Take care in naming the work you enter, so you can locate it again when you want it. Well-named documents preclude frustrating file searches. You'll save the step of bringing the document on-screen to check the contents. Systems vary in the number of letters allowed in naming files. Keep these three tips in mind:

1. Be specific, especially if category names are similar.
2. Be clear, especially if you abbreviate.
3. Be consistent, especially for series of related files

As you create and name files, you must also create places to park them. Remember to identify different versions of the file. For example, differentiate *Allan Pinkerton: The Eye That Never Sleeps* version three (AP.03) from version six (AP.06). Group computer files the way you've divided papers into categories in office file cabinets.

## Organizing Computer Files:
## The Five-Step Computer Management Plan

Do you pile or file in your computer?

If you already have numerous computer files, you may have a mix of files, stored haphazardly. You may have created many directories and subdirectories, but have no organized system. Or you may have separate directories for your programs but, unknowingly, have put all your data in one directory. Or you may have just started and have only a few files. You may be in the same plight as this novice computer owner:

I bought a computer and installed my word-processing program. Then I started "piling" my computer documents the way I do my paper stuff. I haven't taken the time to learn how to organize them into directories and subdirectories. Everything I create goes into one long, long alphabetical mess.

IT MUST BE IN THERE SOMEPLACE!

An overview of a step-by-step approach for gaining control of your computer files is shown below. If you're just starting a new system, you have a clean slate. Go directly to Step 2, but pay attention to the maintenance section of this chapter so you don't end up needing to use the other steps!

## FIVE-STEP COMPUTER MANAGEMENT PLAN

## STEP 1: BACK UP AND DELETE

### Back Up

First do a full disk or tape backup. This is your safety net as you straighten out files you've created and stored. If you delete a file, intentionally or by mistake, and later wish you hadn't, you'll still have a copy.

### Delete

Next prune the deadwood from your computer files. Programs and data you no longer need or want take up memory and clutter your current work.

Skim each of your directories and delete old or irrelevant files, such as work you've changed substantially and saved under a new name, or older files for which you have a hard copy. If you don't recognize the file by its name, view it on the screen to help you decide whether to keep or delete it.

If you find old files you want to move from your hard drive to floppy disk storage, leave them for now. You'll deal with them later in Step 5.

## STEP 2: PLAN AND CREATE DIRECTORIES

Just as you created a File . . . Don't Pile!® blueprint for your paperwork, develop a plan for organizing your computer work. Plan the layout of your computer filing system on paper or on your computer. Make your Computer File Plan meaningful and logical to you.

If you have a file-management program, use it. It allows you to customize the way you organize your files—by date, title, subject, application, and so on.

Both IBM and Mac have a "tree-structured" system for organizing material you save. Much like a genealogy tree, you start with a main category and develop subcategories that branch out from the main trunk. Although the terms used in the systems are different, the storage areas are parallel.

| *IBM System* | *Mac System* |
| --- | --- |
| Root Directory | Desktop |
| Directories | Folders |
| Subdirectories | Files |

Consider storing your computer data in four of the five areas you used to file your writing papers: ***ADMINISTRATIVE, MANUSCRIPTS, MARKETING***, and ***FINANCIAL***. (The fifth area, ***REFERENCE***, may apply only to computer use in special cases.)

Start by writing down these four headings. Then, write or key in the subdirectories (folders) you'll need within each of the areas. Don't extend your directory or folder structure more than three or four layers deep. Based on the *Areas/Categories List* described in Chapter 2, here is how one computer tree might look:

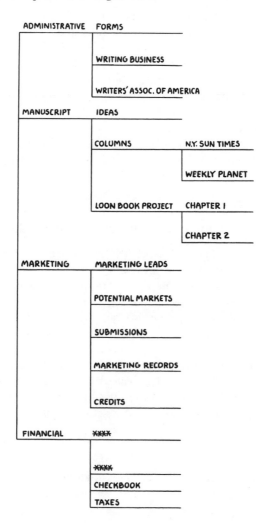

### STEP 3: SET PRIORITIES

If you have a lot of data stored, it may take some time to organize your computer files. Unless you can devote an uninterrupted block of time to the job, set priorities. Decide which directory to organize first, second, and so on. Put your Computer Priorities List with your Master To Do List in your Planning Notebook or post it temporarily near your computer until you finish.

### STEP 4: TAG AND ACT

This step is for already-established files that you want to re-organize. Use your Computer File Plan and Computer Priorities List to guide you.

The Tag function (Mark text or Select) on your computer allows you to mark or highlight file names requiring the same action. If you want to move several files from one directory to another, for instance, a single command moves all tagged files in one fell swoop. You can move tagged files en masse only if they are headed for the same destination. Whether you have minor or major changes to make, tagging simplifies the process.

First, print a hard copy of each of your directories (folders). Some directory listings may be several pages long.

Then, start with the first directory on your priority list. Decide which action you want to take for each file listed for that directory: Keep (K), Move (M), Rename (R), Store (S), or Delete (D). Ask:

- Should I *keep* this file in this directory?
- Should I *move* this file to another directory? If so, which one?
- Should I *rename* this file? If so, what new name?
- Should I *store* this file on a floppy disk?
- Should I *delete* the file?

Pencil the letter for the action next to the file name on your list. If you plan to move the file, pencil in the directory name to which you'll move it. If you want to rename a file, pencil in the new name.

You may have some files that you want to delete from your hard drive, but still store on floppy disks. Pencil in an S for "Store" next to the file name regardless of which directory it's located in now. Store these files temporarily in a directory called ARCHIVE. If you're not sure where to move a file, pencil in the letter H for "Hold" next to the file name. Store these files temporarily in a directory called HOLD. You'll deal with these two directories in Step 5.

### STEP 5: SORT AND STORE

Now deal with the files you have stored in the temporary directory ARCHIVE. These are the files you decided to remove from your hard drive and store on floppy disks. It's best to wait until this step to move these files to the disks. You can tag those you want housed together on the same floppy disk and move them at the same time. After all files in the ARCHIVE directory are stored on your floppy disk, you can delete them from your hard drive.

Finally, look at the files you stored in the directory HOLD. These are the files you were undecided about. Eventually you will need to determine whether you want to store these files on disks, move the files to another directory or subdirectory, or delete them. After you have acted on all the files in this whole directory, you can delete it.

## Maintaining Computer Files

Your computer needs to stay as neat and tidy on the inside as it appears sitting on your desk. (This assumes it isn't peeping through a barrage of Post-it™ Notes or piles of paper!) How do you maintain the files stored deep in your computer's memory?

Like the papers in your file cabinets, keeping computer files organized is an ongoing process. Three actions for maintaining papers—deleting, moving, and protecting—also apply to your computer work.

### DELETING COMPUTER FILES

"Toss" is to paper as "delete" (or "trash") is to computer files.

Every byte of information you key in, whether on hard drive or disk, takes up storage space. If it's been some time since you've purged your computer files, review the deleting process in Step 1 of the Five-Step Computer Management Plan.

Weed your computer files regularly, asking yourself questions like these:

- Will I use this information again?
- Is this document outdated?
- Do I have a stronger, more recent draft?
- Is this past contact valid?
- Is this information still valuable?

## MOVING COMPUTER FILES

Saving past versions allows you to check facts and consistency and to retrieve useful information for inclusion in new work. But storing older and newer versions together can create a jumble in your computer file. Just as you physically move past revisions of a manuscript to a past category, you can create a storage directory, such as MSS/PAST or PAST MANUSCRIPTS, and move past versions of a manuscript there. Or, better still, store them on floppies and delete them from your hard drive.

## PROTECTING COMPUTER FILES

Maintenance also involves protecting what you have from being lost.

In his precomputer days, a blind writer friend hacked out his novels on an old Remington. His worst nightmare, losing what he'd written, came true the time he typed an entire chapter not realizing that the ribbon had worked itself loose. All he had was twenty pockmarked pages. I had the same hollow feeling the day a chapter I'd written got sucked into the Black Hole of my computer.

Follow these three simple rules:

### Rule #1: Save Often

Just as you automatically check your rearview mirror while driving, press your Save key often.

### Rule #2: Know Your Automatic Backup Feature

Some word processors have a built-in "save" function or flash an on-screen "Save now?" message at an interval you determine. As you work, this backup feature tells your computer to save the document as it currently stands. This feature can save you if a power glitch occurs or if you fail to save the document before quitting. You may lose small amounts of work, but most will be saved.

### Rule #3: Back Up and Protect Your Data

Would you want to retype or even *re-create* entire chapters, projects, or books? If you have an automatic save feature in your system, data is saved to your hard drive. But hard drives can fail. Schedule regular floppy or tape backups of all data on your computer at least once a week. This may take time and a number of disks, but it's worth it.

Do a full disk backup for off-site storage once a week. By alternating two sets of disks, you protect yourself against occasional disk corruption and you'll always have a recent full backup.

## Creating and Storing Forms on the Computer

You may opt to create and store generic forms and model correspondence on your computer. Individualize forms for your writing specialty and store them in your ADMINISTRATIVE directory. Instructions and tips for designing forms are included in the Writer's Tool Kit (see order blank at back of book).

One fiction writer developed a standard character analysis form to use when she launches a new project. The form includes space for: physical appearance, personal strengths and weaknesses, preferred clothing, favorite colors, speech patterns, background, occupation, hobbies, and other key factors. She just pulls up this form, and completes a copy for each character in preparation for writing.

Novelist Pam Conrad goes a step further. At the start of each new project, she pulls up a detailed generic form related to the structure of the book. The form includes such specifics as point of view, setting, time, pace and style, theme, one-sentence summary, and more. "About ninety percent of my work on a novel takes place before I start to write," she says.

Not all fiction writers use such a structured model. But if you like to shape your work tightly before you begin, develop an individualized form that suits your style.

## Preparing for Computer-Related Disasters

If your computer lives close to large-voltage electrical equipment—an elevator, motors, or machinery—such watt-guzzlers can cause glitches on your screen or worse. Unexpected power surges in your electrical lines could fry your system. Two devices offer surge protection. The uninterrupted power supply (UPS) is expensive, but will keep your system running during a power failure or "brownout." The other device is a single-function surge protector. It's less expensive and protects your computer from unpredictable voltage spikes.

If needed, you can buy surge protectors to filter out radio frequency interference (RFI) from radio, television, or computer circuitry, and electromagnetic interference (EMI) from high-speed electric motors, fluorescent lights, or photo-optical equipment such as photocopiers.

Modems can also be damaged by electrical spikes and surges. Look for a surge protector that includes phone-line protection.

Computer viruses can erase or replace data or system software files. Most viruses are harmless, but some can be very damaging. Take precautions to defend your data against the many viruses that exist.

For Mac users, an antivirus program is a must. IBM and IBM clones are more resistant to viruses because of the way these systems store files. Do your homework before you buy. (Some antivirus programs have been known to indiscriminately gobble data as well.) Here are some other basic tips:

- Don't share disks (unless you're sure disks are virus free).
- Scan disks with a virus program before using them.
- Keep backups of all computer files.
- Be cautious with free or public domain software. (Generally speaking, commercial software is carefully screened.)
- Check for viruses before downloading from bulletin boards or networks.

In these fast-moving times, brave new worlds continue to open in computer technology. Learning how to use this equipment is one thing, where to put it is another. Chapter 11 looks at efficient ways to design your workspace.

# CHAPTER 11

# Designing the Workspace

## Room at the Top

John Braine

**S**OME writers can work anywhere—on airplanes or commuter trains, at lectures or board meetings, in coffee shops or the doctor's office. Others need a quiet writing place and uninterrupted time.

Finding a spot where the muses can attend you is one thing. Carving out a home base is another. You need a centralized place for storing materials and supplies—a place where you can settle in, spread out, and work.

If you're a "portable" writer, you work wherever you can find space—an empty conference room, a spare room, the dining-room table. When others arrive who need to use the space, you quickly stash your writing materials and vacate. Sound familiar?

I'm a mobile unit . . . I work in three different offices. I constantly have to think of what I'll need where. My car is my office on wheels.

I write in our small living room. When company comes, I stuff my writing papers in bags and hide them. One evening my husband asked me to show our guests something I'd written. Imagine his surprise when I went to the bathroom to get it. He didn't know I'd filed it in the shower!

If you don't have a secure spot to call your own at each location where you work, lobby for one. You may not get the "room at the top," but you deserve some space exclusively for your use.

If you do have a permanent home for your files and supplies, call it your office, whether it's a cubbyhole or a luxury suite. In a small office, fitting files and storage into a compact space poses a challenge.

My office space at the Maritime Museum is quite small and usually filled with brawling drunken sailors and the like (my fellow staffers). I clear them out with a belaying pin and the place suddenly gets much quieter. The space is still too small, but I'm used to that.

With good planning, an effective workspace can be designed in an area as small as six-by-five feet. In fact, with the trend toward teamwork, many traditional private offices are shrinking by as much as 20 percent. This allows more space for conference areas and formal and informal meeting places. But even if your workspace is ample, without careful planning, you may still use a large space inefficiently.

Designing your workspace is the last step in setting up your File . . . Don't Pile!® System. Remember in Chapter 2 how you planned your filing system first so you'd know how much equipment you needed to house your files? It's the same with your workspace. You can't design your workspace unless you know what equipment you want and need to put in that space. You may need to make only minor modifications. But even small changes can make big differences that will save you time and increase your efficiency.

## Reviewing Your Current Office Layout

If you are rearranging or remodeling your current office layout, first review what you have. Here are the basic questions you need to answer. (If you are designing a new office, the first three questions will not apply.)

- Do I have enough space?
- How can I expand my current space?
- How can I make better use of the space I have?
- What are my writing needs?
- What are my filing needs?
- What are my storage needs for books, supplies, and equipment?
- Do I share the office space with others?
- What furniture arrangement is best suited for the space and my needs?
- How can I make filing and storage space convenient?
- What is my work style?
- What image do I want my office to portray?
- What is my budget?

## SKETCH YOUR CURRENT OFFICE

We moved my office—including a 350-pound desk I inherited—to a new location. The desk got plunked down and that's where it stayed. Now I want to rearrange my workspace, but I need to do some serious planning this time. You don't waltz that elephant around the room to decide where it should go!

Start with the basic outline of your office—the perimeter of the space. The truer to scale you draw it and the contents, the easier it will be to move furniture.

Next add fixed features—windows, doorways, outlets, vents, and obstacles such as pipes or radiators. Add storage space, such as built-in cupboards and closets. Finally pencil in your furniture—desk, tables, chairs, file cabinets, credenza, and bookshelves. Some people move scaled, cut-out shapes of furniture around on graph paper to test new arrangements.

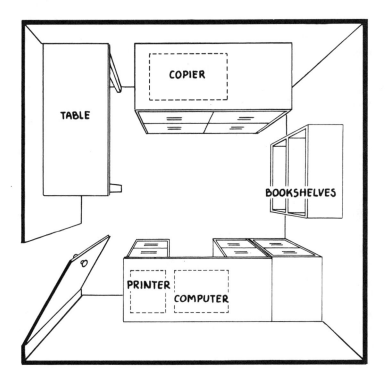

## ASSESS YOUR CURRENT OFFICE LAYOUT

The size and shape of your office affects what you put in it and how you arrange it. If your cubicle has fixed furniture, you must work with a set layout. But where you locate files, supplies, or equipment in that space may make it more efficient. If you have the freedom to shift furniture, you have flexibility in designing a layout to suit your needs. Consider what's important to you.

I knew I needed to change my office layout, but I wasn't sure how. For several days, I thought about how I worked, what I needed, and what I already had. I didn't move a thing until I had thought the whole plan through so I could use the space better.

Do you have any space eaters that can go—a sprawling plant, a bulky storage cupboard with inefficient shelving, a wing-back chair? Could you do without them? Would a smaller, equally appealing or functional replacement serve the same purpose?

I have an electric fireplace in my office that takes up eight square feet. A small ceramic space heater would do the same job and would allow me more room, but it wouldn't seem as cozy.

Place a premium on proper lighting. Is the light in your office conducive to writing or sleeping? Some options for basic room light include ceiling fixtures, track lighting, and long-lasting fluorescent lights. If your office is generally gloomy, a skylight can flood the room with muted light.

My copier is in a dark part of the room, which is bad to start with. Whenever there's a problem with it, I practically have to hold a flashlight in my teeth to make adjustments.

You may need task lighting or undershelf lighting above your printer, copier, and filing areas. Clamp-on or swing lights are inexpensive and illuminate well.

An average office may contain fifteen or more electronic items. Your computer and other hardware need grounded, three-prong outlets. If your office lacks electric outlets, a handy seven-plug power strip can safely remedy the problem without new wiring.

Before the architect drew plans for our office addition, he sketched the present layout and asked about the equipment we currently use. The result? We have an abundance of outlets, which allows great flexibility with lighting and equipment.

Is your office too damp? Dry? Cold? Hot? Noisy? Quiet? Evaluate what you have and need. Think of ways to improve your environment.

My windowless office in the basement had dark wood paneling. A minor modification has worked wonders for my writing environment. I painted the paneling white. It's brighter, seems larger, and I (almost) don't miss having a window.

As you assess your office, the ambience of your work setting is important, too. But beware of sabotaging your own efforts.

I set up an aquarium to add a sense of tranquility to my office. But the books have piled up in front of my restful landscape and I can't see the fish! I'm not even sure they're still in there.

Whether your office is roomy or cramped, the key is having a balance of three types of workspace:

Space to work    Horizontal work surfaces
Space to file    File cabinets or boxes
Space to store   Area for nonpaper items and bulk supplies

You can quickly assess your current office space by doing this simple exercise. Go back to the sketch you drew of your current layout. On the sketch, label your horizontal workspace (*W*), filing space (*F*), and storage space (*S*).

Now analyze your space—what's there and what's lacking. Too few *F*s or *S*s, but plenty of *W*s for instance, might indicate one reason why papers, books, and supplies are piled. There's no place to properly store them. Scarce *W* space might hold the clue to why you end up with your work on your lap.

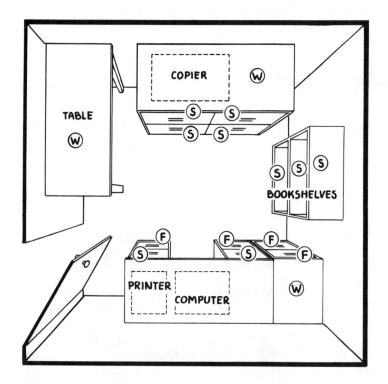

## Creating Space to Work

What space? If there's a horizontal surface, I fill it!

Whatever I'm working on fills the center of my bed and everything fans out from there—books, articles, drafts, mail. . . . Last week's projects go under the bed in new kitty litter boxes.

Your office is the hub of your writing wheel. You won't always work there, but creating the space is a must. You need a place to spread out materials and a place to put equipment.

## ESTABLISH A PLACE TO SPREAD OUT MATERIALS

I need to see the flow of my work, a section at a time. I spread papers out on my office floor. Co-workers sometimes trip over the papers, or I roll my chair over a page.

My work spills out from office to bedroom to kitchen. Papers even pile up on both sides of my dinner plate.

Granted, sometimes you may curl up with a lapboard desk in an armchair to create or edit. But for the long haul, you need a horizontal surface where you can spread out your work—a desk, desk return, table, door across two file cabinets, or counter. (Be sure to allow for leg room.)

Desks vary in style, size, and cost. Be realistic. You may be tempted to save money by buying a smaller desk than you need. A larger one, though, will give you more room to spread out your materials and more places to file. A standard office desktop measures 72 by 36 inches. Some feature a pull-out work surface, much like a breadboard. The height of the desktop from the floor is generally 29 to 30 inches.

Your chair is important, too. Architect Ludwig Mies van der Rohe once said that it was easier to design a skyscraper than a good chair. Shop carefully. Test several desk chairs before you buy. Check each chair's base—it should be broad. A five-prong base offers more stability than a four-prong base. (Crashing over backward is something you want to spoof, not experience.)

Decide whether you want wheels, armrests, and a soft or hard seat. Look for easy adjustments of the chair's back and seat height. Make sure the chair provides good lower-back support. Choosing a good chair can prevent injuries and back strain.

## DESIGNATE A PLACE FOR YOUR EQUIPMENT

The only equipment Thomas Jefferson needed to write the Declaration of Independence was a bottle of ink and a quill pen. Not so today. Machines have revolutionized the modern office.

You may have a computer, printer, answering machine, copier, and more. You need to find homes for this equipment. Here are some possible locations.

### Computer Systems

I used to keep my printer in the corner of my office. But my paper often fell between the wall and the desk and I could only fish for it with a yardstick and tape!

A computer system demands its own space. You can't move your computer, keyboard, and printer every time you need the horizontal surface where they're housed. Designate a permanent home for your system. Measure the components and the space you plan to put them to make sure they fit. Check, too, for outlets. It's harder to read the monitor if you face a window. Your system should be set at a ninety-degree angle to any window. Mini-blinds or light-filtering shades cut outside glare and regulate natural lighting. Filters for monitors are available, too, in mesh or polarized glass.

Rearranging your computer system can give you more of a work area. One writer opened up her computer space by upending the CPU and pushing the printer back toward the wall.

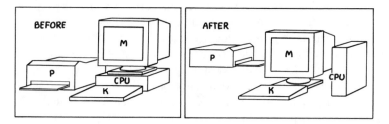

Frequently, the middle pencil drawer of a desk can hold a pull-out keyboard. You can also buy a pull-out keyboard tray that fastens to the underside of a desk.

Unless you share a printer with others, place it close to the computer. If you have a tractor-feed printer, use a stand to allow room for the paper underneath.

Ergonomic experts (who study how people adapt to the workplace), emphasize the importance of adjusting the height of your chair to fit your work surface. Position your monitor so you're looking straight ahead with your chin tilted down slightly. A return (a low table often attached to a desk) provides a good height for a computer. Your feet should be flat on the floor or footrest, your knees slightly higher than your hips.

Repetitive stress injuries, caused by tasks such as keying in data at a computer, are on the rise. Pay close attention to the angle at which your hands meet the keyboard. When you sit in front of your desk or computer keyboard, your elbows should form a right angle. Your hands should rest on the keys at much the same angle, as if you were playing a piano. Fingers, curved slightly, shouldn't be tilting up or reaching down too far to find the keys. If you are of average height, the keyboard should be approximately 25 to 28 inches from the floor. The more you type, the more important this is. Keeping wrists and hands in the most natural position puts less stress on hand, arm, and wrist muscles.

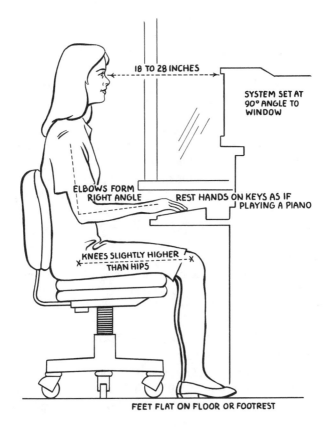

18 TO 28 INCHES

SYSTEM SET AT
90° ANGLE TO
WINDOW

ELBOWS FORM
RIGHT ANGLE

REST HANDS ON KEYS AS IF
PLAYING A PIANO

KNEES SLIGHTLY HIGHER
THAN HIPS

FEET FLAT ON FLOOR OR FOOTREST

Some companies make a keyboard that accommodates the natural position of the hands. This "split wing" model divides a standard keyboard down the middle. Rows of keys on each side angle slightly upward. The pitched keyboard base slopes down and the angled front provides a resting place for wrists.

### Word Processor/Typewriter

I've written three books on my trusty word processor. My writing friends keep urging me to upgrade to a computer. But I know my machine. It works for me. And it fits in the small space where I write.

A word processor takes up less space—about as much as a typewriter—than a computer does. Consider placement, room to spread out materials, and how to position your chair correctly.

If you use a typewriter, factor in the amount of room you need for the carriage return. If your office isn't large enough for the typewriter to have a permanent home, store it nearby until you need it. As you grow into computer technology, you will find less and less use for your typewriter.

I finally put my old electric typewriter away when I learned how to do envelopes and labels on my printer. That's really freed up workspace for me. (This only took me two years!)

### Copier/Answering Machine/FAX

When I bought my copier, I measured the location where I wanted it, but didn't allow room for the moving parts. As a result, I had to rethink my whole office layout to fit it into a new space.

Think about these factors when you position the copier:

* Single or shared usage
* Frequency of use
* Electric outlets
* Lighting
* Room for paper and copier supplies
* Horizontal space nearby to spread out work while copying
* Allowance for moving parts

After repeated attempts to reach one writer, a magazine editor complained, "You must be the last person on earth without an answering machine!"

In this fast-paced world, an answering machine is almost essential. Editors and clients can leave messages. You can count on uninterrupted blocks of writing time. You can screen calls.

Likewise, FAX (Facsimile Transmission) machines are fast (several pages per minute) and provide a vital communication tool. Writers can transmit memos, documents, and whole articles across the country twenty-four hours a day.

Neither the answering machine nor the FAX has to occupy prime work space. Place these machines across the room on a shelf, credenza, or side table.

I wrecked two answering machines because they crashed to the floor whenever I moved the phone. It finally dawned on me that the answering machine didn't have to live right next to the phone. A fifty-foot modular cord let me relocate the machine in a safer spot.

## Creating Space to File

I wish I had a walk-in filing cabinet. What I do have is an overflowing two-drawer file and lots of sagging boxes.

With the groundwork in Chapters 2 through 6 completed, you know what papers you have to file and how. Here's how to choose appropriate containers for storing your categories and how to decide where to put the filing equipment in your office.

## CHOOSE CONTAINERS FOR YOUR FILES

No matter how much filing space you have, you never have enough. Here are three kinds of containers you can use for filing purposes:

- Filing Cabinets
- Crates
- Boxes

### *Filing Cabinets*

When you buy a filing cabinet, decide whether you need letter or legal size. Letter-size cabinets take less space and are less expensive. Most writers work with 8½-by-11-inch paper. But if you sometimes deal with

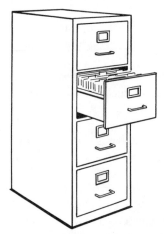

bulky packets or longer paper, you may opt for at least one legal-size cabinet. In either size, make sure drawers have full suspension rollers. With rollers, the drawers will glide open and shut smoothly and effortlessly, even when fully loaded.

The most frequently used type of cabinet is a conventional or vertical unit. You gain about 25 percent more storage room in a five-drawer over a four-drawer size for the same amount of floor space.

Depending on the size and shape of your office, a lateral file may work better for you. Lateral cabinets require less floor space and allow you to file either laterally or front-to-back inside the drawer.

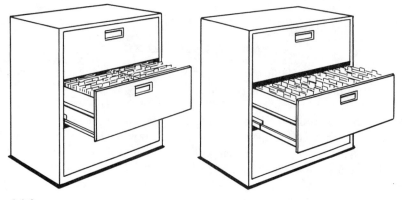

**200**

A file cabinet on casters gives you the option of moving the unit where you need it. One lightweight, portable version features a framework with a closed hanging file crate dropped inside. The crate has a transparent lid for easy viewing. The filing crate lifts out of the frame easily for transporting to another location.

### Crates

Hardware and discount stores carry sturdy open-weave plastic crates, which make great portable files for writers on the move. Collapsible plastic crates store flat and can go 3-D when needed. Be sure to get crates with built-in rails to support hanging folders. When you complete a project, lift the folders from the crate and store them in a box. Use the crate for another hot project.

Some easy-to-carry totes have piano-hinge covers that close tightly with a latch. These are great for transporting materials in bad weather.

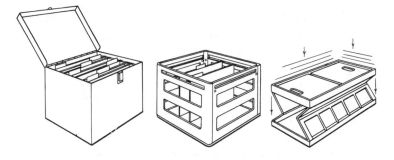

### Boxes

Writers on a shoestring budget can ask the grocer for apple boxes—they're sturdy and clean. Use hanging file frames in slightly larger boxes to create inexpensive file drawers.

You can also buy stackable Bankers™ Boxes or cardboard file drawers. The latter will accommodate hanging file frames.

Remember the exercise you did in Chapter 5 titled "Drawers In and Near Desk—Drawers Away from Desk?" It helped you know which of your categories are pending and which are nonpending. Pull this list; you paper-clipped it in your book.

Make a sketch from this list to show where your pending categories will live. It may look similar to the following drawing:

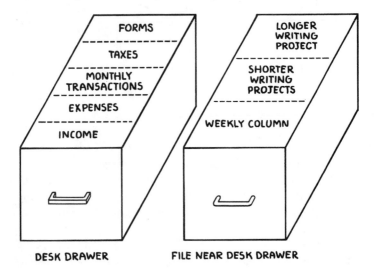

FORMS
TAXES
MONTHLY TRANSACTIONS
EXPENSES
INCOME

LONGER WRITING PROJECT
SHORTER WRITING PROJECTS
WEEKLY COLUMN

DESK DRAWER          FILE NEAR DESK DRAWER

Next, measure the drawer and the actual size of the categories to see how much can fit into the space. This helps you know whether you need to purchase more filing equipment, and whether or not it will fit in the space near your desk.

Repeat this procedure to position the categories listed in the "Drawers Away from Desk" column. Presumably only some of those categories will live in your office. You can house others in storage boxes in an office closet or some other place away from your workspace.

## Creating Space for Storage

For years, the shelf above my computer held a bin of scratch paper (which I didn't need), and an unused computer mouse. My writing books, which I frequently used, lived in a remote bookcase across the room. I finally wised up and replaced the paper and the mouse with my reference books. Now when a writing question comes up while I'm working, the answers are within easy reach.

## ASSESS YOUR STORAGE NEEDS

Writers need space to keep reference books, presentation materials, inventory, and supplies. Determine what and how much you have to store before you buy any new storage containers or units. Here are some items to consider:

### Books and Manuals

Like most writers, you probably have a plethora of books and manuals. Store frequently used reference books such as your dictionary, thesaurus, and grammar books close to where you do your writing. Keep current computer manuals near your system so you can solve on-screen problems quickly.

Put seldom-used books farther away, but make them still accessible. Reserve one section of the bookshelf for sample copies of your own published work. If other books are worth keeping, but don't relate to your current needs, box them up and store them temporarily.

### Supplies

If you work in a business office setting, you may store personal items such as shoes, boots, exercise clothing, food, or hygiene products in a drawer or closet. You may also need hooks for foul-weather gear—a coat, jacket, or umbrella.

Keep small amounts of computer items, paper, and nonpaper supplies in your office. Store bulk computer and office supplies away from your immediate workspace so they don't clutter up your desk or nearby shelves—disks, printer ribbons, tape, paper clips, correction fluid, pens and pencils, yellow pads, Post-its™, staples, envelopes.

### Postal Supplies

You can save many trips to the post office by setting up your own postal center. In a letter tray, drawer, or basket, assemble mailing supplies: stamps, a postal scale or meter, several sizes of mailing envelopes, boxes, padded mailers, a self-inking first-class stamp, a postal-rate chart, International Return Coupons (IRCs), and mailing labels.

### Presentation Materials

If you conduct seminars or teach classes, you may accumulate slides, transparencies, visuals, and participant materials. Store items used exclusively for presentations in portable containers so you don't have to unpack and repack them each time. If you have items you don't use every time, store them in separate boxes.

You've explored the types of containers available. Now where will you store them? Decide what kinds of storage units and how many of them you'll need. Here are some possibilities: built-in or freestanding shelves, bookcases, cabinets (with doors), wall units.

Before you buy, measure the items you're going to store so you won't waste space. Units should be adjustable, versatile, and of a heavy duty material. Practical, no-frills steel shelving and inexpensive Bankers™ boxes are adequate for off-site storage.

## Planning Your Revised Office Layout

In my imagination I dream about having sixty shiny filing cabinets. Not having a big beautiful room to put them in ruins the picture.

As you plan your new office layout, consider your answers to the questions you asked when you reviewed your current office situation. Include the $W$, $F$, and $S$ needs you identified when assessing your office. But you will also want to factor in your work style and some basic principles of organization.

### ACKNOWLEDGE YOUR WORK STYLE

I'm happiest working smack in the main traffic pattern. I've tried working in the basement, but I kept gravitating back to the kitchen table. I was afraid I'd miss something! So I designed a six-foot desk with two file drawers. Attached is a floor-to-ceiling bookcase. Now I can write, hear the faint trill of the Nintendo, monitor what's fair and what's not, and cook soup at the same time.

Ask yourself, where and when am I most productive? What is my tolerance for noise and interruptions? Do I thrive on action or am I frazzled by interference? Am I an early bird or a night owl?

Three basic room arrangements allow you to position yourself either facing toward or away from the action—the U-shape, L-shape, and galley- or corridor-shape. See the illustration on the next page.

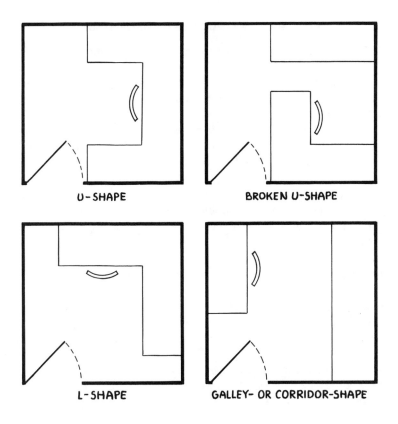

U-SHAPE

BROKEN U-SHAPE

L-SHAPE

GALLEY- OR CORRIDOR-SHAPE

Move a lateral file or credenza at right angles to your desk to create an L-shaped work area. One modification of the U-shape is the broken-U, which has a passageway at the base of the "U" that allows traffic through the area.

Apply the less-is-more theory. Investigate space-saving components, desk returns, library ladders to reach overhead shelves and cupboards, modular furniture systems, and partitions of different heights to provide privacy and a look of spaciousness.

## APPLY BASIC PRINCIPLES OF ORGANIZATION

Keep these three principles in mind when you organize:

### Principle #1: Store Items So You Can See and Retrieve Them

Stacking materials makes them hard to retrieve. Store items vertically or separate them with dividers.

Don't let boxes and piles block access to your file drawers or copier. Obstacles make moving about in your office a life-threatening experience. Leave mountain climbing to the experts.

One day I tripped over a barricade of books and file crates that I had created in my office, fell, and cut my head open. As they stitched up my head at the hospital, I vowed I'd get my act together and get organized.

### Principle #2: Store Items at Point of First Use

Keep paper near the printer, blank transparencies near a copier, disks near the computer, and pending categories in or near your desk. If having three scissors in three locations saves you steps, it warrants having duplicates.

I store my masters in a drawer next to my copier. That way, when I need to make copies of a form or a packet, I can easily pull the originals from my file.

### Principle #3: Store Together Items Used Together

For some weird reason, I kept my disk labels on a shelf in the closet and my disks near the computer. Whenever I copied my column to the disk, I'd have to trek across the room to retrieve a label.

Whether you've revamped your workspace or moved into all-new quarters, understanding your approach to life will give you insight as to why you organize the way you do. Chapter 12 discusses how your personality type affects your organizational style.

# CHAPTER 12
# Understanding Organizational Styles

## As You Like It

William Shakespeare

**E**VER look at people working at their desks and wonder how they can possibly function? Their desks are *too* neat. *Too* messy.

Every day you unconsciously make choices. As *you* like it! You don't often think about your options. They are so familiar and comfortable they've become automatic.

This chapter shows how the choices you make affect your organizational style—particularly as the choices relate to paper.

Try this experiment. Write your signature as if you were signing a check. Now switch hands and write it again—as freely and flowingly as you did the first time. "Flowingly?" you say, laughing.

How did you feel the second time? Awkward? Did you have to concentrate harder? Unless you're ambidextrous, you felt more comfortable writing your name the first time than the second. But you *could* do it. If you lose the use of your preferred hand, you probably could manage with the other.

Learning about personality type provides a framework so you can gain new insight as to how and why you organize paper as you do. Use this chapter as an introduction to the Myers-Briggs Type Indicator® (MBTI®).

## Understanding Type

The MBTI® is one of many recognized psychological questionnaires. It is used by educators, management consultants, career counselors, psychologists, therapists, and psychoanalysts. Isabel Briggs Myers and her mother, Katharine C. Briggs, created the MBTI® after twenty years of research and development.

The MBTI® measures characteristics and tendencies of people's personalities as defined by Swiss psychiatrist Carl Jung. According to the instrument, your preferences in four basic categories determine your psychological type. Each category has two choices. Every day you use all eight possibilities to some degree. But just as you prefer right-handedness or left-handedness, you usually favor one preference in each pair from the four categories.

Sandra Hirsh and Jean Kummerow, authors of *LifeTypes*, describe the categories as shown in the chart on the next page.

## Determining Your Type

To understand why you act the way you do when it comes to filing and/ or piling paper, you must first understand who *you* are. It may be possible to determine your personality type by simply reading books on the topic. The reliable method is to take the MBTI® from a qualified person trained to interpret it and to give counseling based on the results.

On pages 212 and 213 are descriptive phrases for each preference. There are no right or wrong preferences. Keep this observation from the MBTI® in mind:

> Whatever your preferences ... you may still use some behavioral characteristics of contrasting preferences, *but not with equal liking* ... [emphasis added].

The chart on pages 214 and 215 provides "thumbnail" profiles of the sixteen general personality types on the MBTI®. As you read the brief description for your probable type, bear in mind that the MBTI® is only one piece of information in determining your type—not the final authority. Only *you* can validate your type. Other factors, as discussed on page 226, also should be considered.

What happens if you can't decide what type you are? Don't be concerned. After you have had some time to absorb the definitions of each preference and observe how each behaves, type usually becomes clear.

## 1. Energizing Preferences

(How and where you get your energy . . .)

(E) *Extraversion*\*  You draw energy from the external world of people, activities, and things.

(I) *Introversion*  You draw energy from the inner world of ideas, emotions, and impressions.

## 2. Attending Preferences

(What you pay attention to when you gather information . . .)

(S) *Sensing*  You focus on what actually exists and pay attention to information perceived directly through the five senses.

(N) *Intuition*  You focus on what might or could be and pay attention to information taken in through a "sixth sense."

## 3. Deciding Preferences

(What system you use when you decide . . .)

(T) *Thinking*  You relate to making decisions based on logic and objectivity.

(F) *Feeling*  You relate to making decisions based on people's needs and on personal values.

## 4. Living Preferences

(What type of life-style you adopt . . .)

(J) *Judging*  You relate to living a planned and organized life.

(P) *Perceptive*  You relate to living a spontaneous, flexible life.

   Letter codes are used to represent the preferences: **E** for Extraversion, **I** for Introversion, **S** for Sensing, **N** for Intuition, **T** for Thinking, **F** for feeling, **J** for Judging, and **P** for Perception. (Note that because **I** is used for Introversion, **N** is used for Intuition to avoid confusion.)

\* Extraversion is correct MBTI® spelling.

## E  EXTRAVERT                    I  INTROVERT

*(How and where you get your energy ...)*

| | |
|---|---|
| *If you are an extravert, you tend to:* | *If you are an introvert, you tend to:* |

| | |
|---|---|
| • prefer the outer world of action | • prefer the inner world of reflection |
| • be expressive; easier to know | • be quiet; harder to know |
| • share emotions, opinions, and experiences | • control emotions; withhold opinions |
| • act and speak before thinking | • think before acting and speaking |
| • plunge into new experiences | • exercise caution with new experiences |
| • check out others' standards | • set own standards when possible |
| • focus on people and things; are sociable | • focus on ideas, concepts; are reserved |
| • need relationships; work with others | • need privacy; work alone or with one person |
| • not mind distractions or interruptions | • like peace and quiet |

## S  SENSING                     N  INTUITIVE

*(What you pay attention to when you gather information ...)*

| | |
|---|---|
| *If you prefer sensing, you tend to:* | *If you prefer intuition, you tend to:* |

| | |
|---|---|
| • process information sequentially | • process information randomly |
| • like directions, rules | • dislike directions, rules |
| • like routine, repetition; dislike change | • like variety; dislike routine |
| • be practical, factual | • be imaginative, creative |
| • live in present | • live in future |
| • deal with concrete issues | • deal with abstract issues |
| • be detail-oriented; read "fine print" | • be big-picture oriented; see patterns |
| • operate "with perspiration," be the doer | • operate "with inspiration," be the innovator |
| • finish projects, but not always initiate the ideas | • initiate ideas, but not always finish the projects |

212

## T  THINKING

### F  FEELING

*(What system you use when you decide . . .)*

*If you prefer thinking,*
*you tend to:*
- base decisions on logic and principles
- analyze
- trust intellect
- communicate in brief, businesslike manner
- value truth and justice

- appear detached with people
- evaluate objectively
- critique
- use rationale to convince

*If you prefer feeling,*
*you tend to:*
- base decisions on personal values and people's needs
- empathize
- trust emotions
- communicate in a talkative, personal manner
- value relationships and harmony
- appear caring with people
- evaluate subjectively
- appreciate
- use persuasion to convince


## J  JUDGING

### P  PERCEPTIVE

*(What type of life-style you adopt . . .)*

*If you are a judging type,*
*you tend to:*
- prefer being organized and systematic
- use time in a deliberate and structured manner
- adhere to deadlines and plan ahead
- decide quickly, closing out further options
- approach new situations hesitantly; maintain first impressions
- like rules and regulations
- form settled opinions that become "shoulds" and "oughts"
- persevere
- dislike interruptions

*If you are a perceptive type,*
*you tend to:*
- prefer being flexible and adaptable
- use time in a "go with the flow," spontaneous manner
- stretch deadlines and allow the future to happen
- decide tentatively, leaving options open
- approach new situations curiously with open mind
- dislike rules and regulations
- be understanding and uncritical
- postpone
- welcome the unexpected

**213**

# CHARACTERISTICS FREQUENTLY ASSOCIATED WITH EACH TYPE

## SENSING TYPES

| | WITH THINKING | WITH FEELING |
|---|---|---|
| **INTROVERTS — JUDGING** | **ISTJ**<br>Serious, quiet, earn success by concentration and thoroughness. Practical, orderly, matter-of-fact, logical, realistic and dependable. See to it that everything is well organized. Take responsibility. Make up their own minds as to what should be accomplished and work toward it steadily, regardless of protests or distractions.<br>Live their outer life more with thinking, inner more with sensing. | **ISFJ**<br>Quiet, friendly, responsible and conscientious. Work devotedly to meet their obligations. Lend stability to any project or group. Thorough, painstaking, accurate. May need time to master technical subjects, as their interests are not often technical. Patient with detail and routine. Loyal, considerate, concerned with how other people feel.<br>Live their outer life more with feeling, inner more with sensing. |
| **INTROVERTS — PERCEPTIVE** | **ISTP**<br>Cool onlookers, quiet, reserved, observing and analyzing life with detached curiosity and unexpected flashes of original humor. Usually interested in impersonal principles, cause and effect, or how and why mechanical things work. Exert themselves no more than they think necessary, because any waste of energy would be inefficient.<br>Live their outer life more with sensing, inner more with thinking. | **ISFP**<br>Retiring, quietly friendly, sensitive, modest about their abilities. Shun disagreements, do not force their opinions or values on others. Usually do not care to lead but are often loyal followers. May be rather relaxed about assignments or getting things done, because they enjoy the present moment and do not want to spoil it by undue haste or exertion.<br>Live their outer life more with sensing, inner more with feeling. |
| **EXTRAVERTS — PERCEPTIVE** | **ESTP**<br>Matter-of-fact, do not worry or hurry, enjoy whatever comes along. Tend to like mechanical things and sports, with friends on the side. May be a bit blunt or insensitive. Adaptable, tolerant, generally conservative in values. Dislike long explanations. Are best with real things that can be worked, handled, taken apart or put back together.<br>Live their outer life more with sensing, inner more with thinking. | **ESFP**<br>Outgoing, easygoing, accepting, friendly, fond of a good time. Like sports and making things. Know what's going on and join in eagerly. Find remembering facts easier than mastering theories. Are best in situations that need sound common sense and practical ability with people as well as with things.<br>Live their outer life more with sensing, inner more with feeling. |
| **EXTRAVERTS — JUDGING** | **ESTJ**<br>Practical realists, matter-of-fact, with a natural head for business or mechanics. Not interested in subjects they see no use for, but can apply themselves when necessary. Like to organize and run activities. Tend to run things well, especially if they remember to consider other people's feelings and points of view when making their decisions.<br>Live their outer life more with thinking, inner more with sensing. | **ESFJ**<br>Warm-hearted, talkative, popular, conscientious, born cooperators, active committee members. Always doing something nice for someone. Work best with plenty of encouragement and praise. Little interest in abstract thinking or technical subjects. Main interest is in things that directly and visibly affect people's lives.<br>Live their outer life more with feeling, inner more with sensing. |

|  WITH FEELING | WITH THINKING |
| --- | --- |
| **INFJ**<br>Succeed by perseverance, originality and desire to do whatever is needed or wanted. Put their best efforts into their work. Quietly forceful, conscientious, concerned for others. Respected for their firm principles. Likely to be honored and followed for their clear convictions as to how best to serve the common good.<br>Live their outer life more with feeling, inner more with intuition. | **INTJ**<br>Have original minds and great drive which they use only for their own purposes. In fields that appeal to them they have a fine power to organize a job and carry it through with or without help. Skeptical, critical, independent, determined, often stubborn. Must learn to yield less important points in order to win the most important.<br>Live their outer life more with thinking, inner more with intuition. |
| **INFP**<br>Full of enthusiasms and loyalties, but seldom talk of these until they know you well. Care about learning, ideas, language, and independent projects of their own. Apt to be on yearbook staff, perhaps as editor. Tend to undertake too much, then somehow get it done. Friendly, but often too absorbed in what they are doing to be sociable or notice much.<br>Live their outer life more with intuition, inner more with feeling. | **INTP**<br>Quiet, reserved, impersonal. Enjoy especially theoretical or scientific subjects. Logical to the point of hair-splitting. Interested mainly in ideas, with little liking for parties or small talk. Tend to have very sharply defined interests. Need to choose careers where some strong interest of theirs can be used and useful.<br>Live their outer life more with intuition, inner more with thinking. |
| **ENFP**<br>Warmly enthusiastic, high-spirited, ingenious, imaginative. Able to do almost anything that interests them. Quick with a solution for any difficulty and ready to help anyone with a problem. Often rely on their ability to improvise instead of preparing in advance. Can always find compelling reasons for whatever they want.<br>Live their outer life more with intuition, inner more with feeling. | **ENTP**<br>Quick, ingenious, good at many things. Stimulating company, alert and outspoken, argue for fun on either side of a question. Resourceful in solving new and challenging problems, but may neglect routine assignments. Turn to one new interest after another. Can always find logical reasons for whatever they want.<br>Live their outer life more with intuition, inner more with thinking. |
| **ENFJ**<br>Responsive and responsible. Feel real concern for what others think and want, and try to handle things with due regard for other people's feelings. Can present a proposal or lead a group discussion with ease and tact. Sociable, popular, sympathetic. Responsive to praise and criticism.<br>Live their outer life more with feeling, inner more with intuition. | **ENTJ**<br>Hearty, frank, decisive, leaders in activities. Usually good in anything that requires reasoning and intelligent talk, such as public speaking. Are well-informed and keep adding to their fund of knowledge. May sometimes be more positive and confident than their experience in an area warrants.<br>Live their outer life more with intuition, inner more with thinking. |

JUDGING

PERCEPTIVE

PERCEPTIVE

JUDGING

INTROVERTS

EXTRAVERTS

## Applying Type to Organizational Style

Writers may be *any* of the sixteen types. Some studies indicate, however, that writers are more often intuitive (N) than sensing (S). In fact, more writers tend to be NPs than any other preference.

Knowing your type doesn't explain everything about how you operate, but it can offer possible reasons for certain organizing problems. With this awareness, you can change old habits and develop new ones.

The Organizational Style Charts on pages 218–225 list some common tendencies of these four combinations—SJ, SP, NJ, NP—and brief profiles as related to paperwork and filing.

The Sensing/Intuition (S/N) and Judging/Perceptive (J/P) preferences have a major impact on how you approach organization. But take into consideration that your Thinking/Feeling (T/F) preference also influences your organizational style. If you prefer Thinking, you base your decisions for managing paper on logic. If you prefer Feeling, you base your decisions on the emotional value you place on the paper.

The organizational charts focus on the following issues:

- How you decide what to save, file, or toss
- What motivates you to file
- How you create a system that works for you
- How you implement the system
- How you maintain the system once it's in place

## Getting Filing Help from Other Types

If you are an extravert (E), you may want another person with you when you tackle your filing project because you think best when talking. It seems easier to plan categories when you can discuss them.

If you are an introvert (I), you are likely to want to be alone when you set up your system because you think best when you consider problems by yourself. For you, it's more comfortable to plan your system in solitude. You don't want to make a party of filing the way extraverts might.

If you are an intuitive (N), a sensing type can keep you from getting sidetracked because his or her perception of reality is different. Sensors are better at seeing what is; intuitives, at seeing what could be. When you discover a long-forgotten paper and are off in Never Never Land reminiscing or dreaming up new possibilities, a sensor will bring you back to earth. But find a sensor who values your priorities and appreciates your frequent spin-offs. A reality-based sensing type will understand that the task at hand is to organize, not to create.

If you are a sensor (S), an intuitive can help you see the big picture instead of being mired in detail. An intuitive can suggest multiple possibilities for how your papers can be used and filed. In filing, an intuitive is the telescope to the sensor's microscope.

If you are a thinking type (T), a feeling type can help you understand the value in your papers before you decide to toss them. You might discard a short excerpt as worthless, but a person with a feeling preference can help you identify the human side of it that draws the reader in. Even a scribbled note can trigger a rich story line that your readers will understand and appreciate.

If you are a feeling type (F), a thinking type can help you view your papers objectively. You see your treasures as "friends," a trail of memories. Someone with a thinking preference can help you develop a structure so that you can make less personal decisions about what to save or toss.

If you are a perceptive type (P), a person with a judging preference can help you make decisions about your categories. You may not be ready to permanently fix your papers in a category because that limits their potential. Cross-referencing allows you to acknowledge all of the possibilities.

If you are a judging type (J), a perceptive type can prevent you from throwing papers away too quickly, just to make a decision. Perceptive types can also help you keep the door open as new ideas and categories emerge.

# SJ (Sensing/Judging)
## Organizational Style Chart

••••••••••••••••••••••••••••••••••••••••••••••••••••••••••••••••••••••

*As a Sensing/Judging type, you . . .*

**Deciding to save or toss**
- Believe it's your responsibility to save and organize materials from the past
- Save information because you don't want to rely on others for it
- Save papers to prove or document facts

**Motivating self to file**
- Have a driving need to have your desk and files in control, neat and orderly
- Want to continually refine your files
- Are pleased to be able to access information quickly

**Creating a system**
- Want a clear, well-defined system spelled out for you rather than having to create one from scratch
- Want a practical system that uses common sense
- Have overly detailed and thorough categories

**Setting up and finishing the system**
- Put task on a "to do" list and systematically work on it without getting sidetracked
- Want uninterrupted blocks of time to work on setting up files
- Need closure—will work on the filing project until it is completed

**Maintaining the system**
- Want desk and files to *stay* organized so dutifully refile folders after use
- Include maintaining the system as part of routine activities
- Have a plentiful stock of filing supplies on hand

## PROFILE OF AN SJ

The strength of SJs is their ability to finish efficiently and consistently what they start. They are the royalty of follow-up. With their well-ordered schedules, you can always count on them to be on time or early for any deadline.

What throws SJs is unplanned change. Change of rules. Change of systems. When others miss their deadlines and disrupt an SJ's ordered life, it's upsetting. They tend to complain a lot if an alternate plan is announced after a decision has been made, but once SJs are converted to a new idea, they'll follow it loyally.

Although SJs are naturally organized, dreaming up a filing system isn't particularly easy (or fun) for them. "I work best with ideas I can *see*," an SJ remarked. "I rely on manuals others have written. Let *them* figure out the instructions." The use of color in a system appeals to them.

For SJs, moving forward is based on present needs. That's why it's difficult for SJs to foresee other uses for their papers or categories. Says one SJ, "My categories are very clearly defined. I seldom use cross-references. I file the papers under the subjects they belong in and what they're used for "

# SP (Sensing/Perceptive)
## Organizational Style Chart

*As a Sensing/Perceptive type, you ...*

**Deciding to save or toss**
- Save more than necessary so you aren't missing pertinent data
- Save papers if they have practical application to your current projects
- Dislike making decisions about what to throw away

**Motivating self to file**
- Want to have quick access to a wide variety of information
- Will establish a system if it means you have more freedom to do what you want to do
- Will file if it isn't mandatory

**Creating a system**
- Want a system that is easy to understand
- Want a system that is practical and makes sense
- Like a system to be comprehensive and cross-referenced

**Setting up and finishing the system**
- Want a system that is simple to set up
- Want the system functioning as quickly as possible
- Will finish task if committed to it and make it a priority

**Maintaining the system**
- Maintain system if it isn't time consuming
- May have difficulty maintaining files when focus of attention shifts to new interests
- Maintain the system when the spirit moves you

### PROFILE OF AN SP

SPs are very attuned to current reality and are good at troubleshooting and negotiating. A flagging newspaper would do well to hire an SP editor, a person to be counted on in a crisis. When SPs want to do something, they do it and get it done.

When others dictate orders, SPs demand freedom to do their own thing. They are action-oriented people. Their filing system needs to be simple and easy to set up. This leaves them free to participate in the activities that are important to them.

SPs don't like organizing and structuring themselves so much as they do collecting more information. They tend to save more than is useful to them. One avid angler, who makes her living writing articles and books about fishing, subscribes to seventeen fishing publications, has maps of every fishing lake, pond, and stream in the state, and has two four-drawer file cabinets filled with reference articles. Of all these materials, she says, "It's great stuff! Occasionally I might look at it. But, I'm usually out in the boat or on the dock. I spend a lot of time talking with others."

How *do* they keep up with it all? They don't. Even if an SP "buys into" a filing system, part of the agreement is not having to be tied down to maintain it. An SP technical writer says, "Once in a while, if I'm in the mood, I'll spend a few minutes and poke around in my files. But they're pretty much on their own. I know they're not going anywhere."

# NJ (Intuitive/Judging)
## Organizational Style Chart

*As an Intuitive/Judging type, you ...*

**Deciding to save or toss**
- Base decision to save or toss paper on its potential uses
- Have creative, intuitive insights as to how items might fit into the "big picture"
- Tend to toss papers when in a "pitching" mood

**Motivating self to file**
- Tie the need to organize into a larger goal with future benefits
- Want your environment to be under control
- Know that it is easier to find items if filed

**Creating a system**
- Create your own system or adapt others' ideas to suit your needs
- Approach the task with a global view of the entire system
- Want an uncomplicated system that can be set up quickly

**Setting up and finishing the system**
- Assess what needs to be done and organize project before starting
- May get sidetracked "midstream"
- Want project ultimately done, so find a way to complete it

**Maintaining the system**
- Attend to files in spurts of enthusiasm
- Maintain system as long as it intuitively makes sense to you
- Keep up because you enjoy reducing clutter

## PROFILE OF AN NJ

NJs are able to visualize globally and make decisions easily. They can identify how papers could fit into future projects and can determine where to file the papers.

The difficulty NJs experience is inconsistency. They are wonderful organizers, but it's usually on a hot-cold basis. They tend to file in spurts. Says one typical NJ, "I let a mess go a day or two and then I go nuts organizing. My office stays neat for a week. Then, I'm in a mess again."

The intuitive nature of an NJ sidetracks them. This can happen before, during, or after their bursts of energy. As a result, NJs might stop to read a magazine article or nostalgic letter in the midst of organizing a drawer. An NJ poet says, "I sit on the floor amongst my piles and spend hours cogitating all the precious things I've kept. Then the phone rings or some other interruption occurs. I'm forced to moved ahead on a deadline. Three or four weeks later, I begin anew."

Of these four organizational styles—SJ, SP, NJ, NP—the NJs suffer the most with their piles and messy files. The two preferences, N and J, are in conflict with each other. The intuitive in them wants variety and creativity, while their judging preference cries out for order and closure. One NJ remarks, "Sometimes I feel like Alice in *Alice in Wonderland*. Part of her longed for the order of her real world and part of her gravitated toward the fantasy of her imaginary world."

# NP (Intuitive/Perceptive)
## Organizational Style Chart

*As an Intuitive Perceptive type, you . . .*

**Deciding to save or toss**
- Have the philosophy of "I might find a use for that someday"
- See endless possibilities and potential in your papers and books
- Toss no paper "before its time"

**Motivating self to file**
- Must see real benefits in the future for setting up system
- May try a system just because it's a new approach
- May set up system if outside events demand it

**Creating a system**
- Want a broad cross-referenced system to allow for all possible uses of information
- May start several systems operating simultaneously
- Seek many ideas continually on how to get organized

**Setting up and finishing the system**
- Work with bursts of energy
- Regard filing as an ongoing, often tedious, process
- May have difficulty finishing the system setup unless you have someone to assist you in staying on track

**Maintaining the system**
- Need frequent remotivation to see real benefit
- Find it difficult to stick with maintenance when challenge is gone and filing becomes routine
- Maintain in spurts of enthusiasm

## PROFILE OF AN NP

NPs find expressing imaginative ideas easy. With their creativity and spontaneity, they see endless possibilities in everything around them. Visualizing concepts is as natural to them as breathing.

But, these same characteristics often cause disorder in their lives. Like NJs, it's very easy for NPs to get sidetracked and distracted when the sparkle of a new idea comes along. To an intuitive, beginnings are a driving force. It's been said that the NP's motto is: "We've only just begun, begun, begun." What usually gets left in the wake are partially completed manuscripts, open books, and piles of notes.

Any little idea may serve as an inspiration, which is one reason why NPs tend to "save it all" and let paper accumulate. An NP writer explains: "My roommate announced that my office in our new house would have no desk. Puzzled, I asked why. The reply was, 'We're going to furnish that room with a pillow on the floor, a telephone, and your piles!' To maintain our sanity, we now have rules about my piles—where they can be and how high."

This doesn't imply that NPs don't have priorities. They do. But it's sometimes difficult for others to see them. That's because NPs tend to create *internal* order out of chaos around them. "Don't touch anything on my desk! I know where everything is." Often they do. As one NP says: "I wish I had the kind of fileless nose I.F. Stone had. He was in the business of putting out one of the best newsletters in the country and never had time to file. But, he knew instinctively where certain items could be found."

NPs tend to vacillate between being overwhelmed by and oblivious to their ceiling-high stacks. Often it isn't until a work surface is needed that prompts them to move the magazines or papers. *Where* the piles are moved is another matter. Says one NP, "Unless I need to use the dining-room table for dinner guests, I'm only dimly aware that it's full of papers. It isn't until I need space on a counter that I clear off the books."

But, NPs can get tripped up if they have too many irons in the fire or must bulldoze through piles to find an important paper. A technical writer for a major corporation was horrified when she unearthed a terse second reminder about a missed deadline. An NP textbook writer desperately searched for a $6,000 cashier's check she knew she'd stashed in a safe, flat place. She found it four months later tucked under the dining-room tablecloth.

## Factoring in Other Influences

Those trained in the professional use of the MBTI® don't use type to label people or to lock them into boxes, but to help them recognize and understand everyone as complex individuals with unique characteristics.

The MBTI® can be approached on many different levels. There are variables within each type. You may find fellow writers who are the same general type but differ greatly from one another. It depends on how strong a preference each writer has for the various characteristics. The MBTI® is not intended to compare you to others. It simply reports how *clearly* you responded concerning your preferences.

Another factor to consider is whether others have nurtured or negated your preferred style throughout your life. Your natural style of organization may or may not be the same as others in your family. One NP writer says: "Although I am an NP, I have SJ skills because of having been raised by an SJ mother. My NP daughter doesn't have those SJ skills because she was raised by an NP."

Susan Scanlon, in her newsletter, *The Type Reporter*, explains what can happen after some people first learn about their type.

[Some] want to head full force in that direction. One man said, "It's like finally finding your dream house. Once you're in it, you know you're not going to be moving or adding on for a while." But for others, the first question they ask is: "If I'm intuitive, can I learn to be more sensing?" or "If I'm a thinking type, how can I develop my feeling [side]?"

Learning to develop and use the abilities that come naturally to people of the opposite preference will help you create a balance. Not only will you become more organized, but you'll be a more effective writer.

Knowing about type can increase your awareness of yourself and improve your understanding of others. Type provides clues for the most effective way to learn the skills you need for everyday living. The fresh perspective you gain from this knowledge can help you solve problems, choose a career, manage a business, or teach students.

## Learning More About Type

Psychologists and educators have spent many years of research carefully developing the psychological type theory. For more information concerning psychological type, see the resources listed in the back of the book or contact these organizations:

Center for Applications of Psychological Type (CAPT)
2720 NW 6th Street
Gainesville, Florida 32609
1-800-777-2278

Association for Psychological Type (APT)
9140 Ward Parkway
Kansas City, Missouri 64114
1-816-444-3500

Consulting Psychologists Press (CPP)
3803 East Bayshore Road
Palo Alto, California 94303
1-800-624-1765

The File . . . Don't Pile!® System is not a panacea for all organizational woes. But its flexibility appeals to people of various personality types, no matter what the approach to filing has been in the past. Feeling comfortable with your own personal preferences will help you to adapt the System to your own needs.

Now some final words of encouragement . . .

# Epilogue

## This Side of Paradise

F. Scott Fitzgerald

**P**ICTURE it. A peace-filled setting.

A place where you can muse, think, write. *And* find the papers you need.

Sound like paradise?

Perhaps, if that's how you picture paradise. Does this mean all paper clips face east in your dream office? Maybe not. Remember, your personality plays a major role in your organizational style. *This Side of Paradise* to you may be *Paradise Lost* to someone else.

Imagining paradise is one thing. Getting there is another. Think back to what prompted you to buy this book:

- Lost checks
- Missed deadlines
- New Year's resolutions
- Comments of others
- Time-wasting searches
- Misplaced papers

What motivates you to progress beyond "good intentions" to getting organized? You may say to yourself, "I don't want to be in this same chaos two years from now!"

An impending move to a smaller house prompted one writer to get serious about his teetering stacks of papers and magazines.

For another writer, reality struck with a newspaper feature:

An interviewer snapped a photo of me holding my new book in my office. When the picture appeared, I saw for the first time the jumble of papers that surrounded me.

Sometimes a tougher jolt causes the light to dawn. A life-threatening accident firmed one writer's resolve to set up a filing system. An avalanche of paperwork from doctors, lawyers, and insurance companies poured into her pack-rat environment.

Whatever motivates you, *File ... Don't Pile!® For People Who Write* can help you gain control of your papers. Will setting up your filing system happen in one day? One weekend? Probably not. It took you longer than forty-eight hours to create that wonderful mess, didn't it? Don't let the volume of clutter overwhelm you. The Five-Step Organization Plan gets you rolling. Tackle what's most important to you first. Will you get sidetracked? No doubt.

I know from past experience that things will get discombobulated again. But now, each time, I see progress. I'm spiraling—gradually getting more organized. I'm in charge of the paper. It doesn't rule me.

The key is moving forward. One pile at a time. One category at a time. One drawer at a time. You can do it! Plutarch, the first-century Greek biographer, said it well and truly:

Many things which cannot be overcome when they are together yield themselves up when taken little by little.

# RESOURCES

## Paper Management

Bennick, Ann. *Filing and Records Management Fundamentals for the Small Business.* Prairie Village, Ks.: Association of Records Managers and Administrators (ARMA), 1987.

Booher, Dianna. *Cutting Paperwork in the Corporate Culture.* New York: Facts on File Publications, 1986.

Dorff, Pat. *File . . . Don't Pile!®* New York: St. Martin's Press, 1986.

Ricks, Betty, Ann J. Swafford, and Kay F. Gow. *Information and Image Management.* 3rd ed. Cincinnati, Oh.: South-Western Publishing Co., 1992.

Robek, Mary F., Gerald F. Brown, and Wilmer Maedke. *Information and Records Management.* 3rd ed. Mission Hills, Calif.: Glencoe/McGraw-Hill, 1987.

Skupsky, Donald S. *Recordkeeping Requirement; The First Practical Guide to Help You Control Your Records . . . What You Need to Keep and What You Can Safely Destroy!* Denver, Co.: Information Requirements Clearinghouse, 1988.

————. *Records Retention Procedures; Your Guide to Determine How Long to Keep Your Records and How to Safely Destroy Them.* Denver, Co.: Information Requirements Clearinghouse, 1991.

## Psychological Type

Brownsword, Alan. *Psychological Type: An Introduction.* Gainesville, Fla.: Center for Applications of Psychological Type, 1988.

Hirsh, Sandra and Jean Kummerow. *LifeTypes.* New York: Warner Publications, 1989.

Jensen, George H. and John K. DiTiberio. *Personality and the Teaching of Composition.* Norwood, N.J.: Ablex Publishing Co., 1989.

Keirsey, David W. and Marilyn Bates. *Please Understand Me.* Del Mar, Calif.: Promethean, 1978.

Kroger, Otto and Janet M. Thuesen. *Type Talk.* New York: Delacorte Press, 1988.

Myers, Isabel Briggs and Peter Briggs Myers. *Gifts Differing.* Palo Alto, Calif.: Consulting Psychologists Press, Inc., 1980.

Scanlon, Susan, ed. "The Type Reporter." Newsletter published eight times a year by The Type Reporter, Inc., 524 N. Paxton St, Alexandria, Virginia 22304.

# Writing

Brande, Dorothea. *Becoming a Writer.* Los Angeles, Calif.: J. P. Tarcher, 1981.

Cheney, Theodore A. Rees. *Getting the Words Right.* Cincinnati, Oh.: Writer's Digest, 1983.

Gardner, John. *The Art of Fiction.* New York: Vintage Books, 1963.

Goldberg, Natalie. *Writing Down the Bones: Freeing the Writer Within.* Boston, Mass.: Shambhala, 1986.

Provost, Gary. *Beyond Style.* Cincinnati, Oh.: Writer's Digest Books, 1988.

Rico, Gabriele Lusser. *Writing the Natural Way.* Los Angeles, Calif.: J. P. Tarcher Inc., 1983.

Welty, Eudora. *One Writer's Beginnings.* Cambridge, Mass.: Harvard University Press, 1984.

*Writer's Digest* magazine. Writer's Digest, 1507 Dana Ave., Cincinnati, Oh. 45207.

*The Writer* magazine. The Writer, 120 Boylston St., Boston, Mass. 02116.

Zinsser, William. *On Writing Well.* New York: Harper and Row, 1985.

# Writing Reference

*The Chicago Manual of Style.* Chicago: The University of Chicago Press, 1993.

French, Christopher W., ed. *The Associated Press Stylebook and Libel Manual.* New York: Dell Publishing (Laurel Book), 1987.

Skillen, Marjorie E. *Words Into Type.* 4th ed. Englewood Cliffs, N.J.: Prentice-Hall, Inc., 1994.

Strunk, William Jr. and E. B. White. *The Elements of Style.* 3rd ed. New York: Collier Macmillan, 1979.

*Webster's New World Misspeller's Dictionary.* New York: Simon and Schuster, 1983.

# Words

Byrne, Josefa Heifetz. *Mrs. Byrne's Dictionary of Unusual, Obscure and Preposterous Words.* Secaucus, N.J.: University Books Citadel Press, 1974.

Ehrlich, Eugene. *Amo, Amas, Amat.* New York: Harper, Collins, 1987.

Martin, Phyllis. *Word Watcher's Handbook, A Deletionary of the Most Abused and Misused Words.* 3rd ed. New York: St. Martin's Press, 1991.

Rodale, J. I. *The Synonym Finder.* Emmaus, Penn.: Rodale Press, 1978.

Thomas, Lewis. *Et Cetera, Et Cetera: Notes of a Word-Watcher.* New York: Penguin Books, 1990.

Urdang, Laurence, ed. *The New York Times Everyday Reader's Dictionary of Misunderstood, Misused, and Mispronounced Words.* New York: Times Books (Random House), 1985.

# Grammar

Baugh, L. Sue. *Essentials of English Grammar*. Lincolnwood, IL: Passport Books, 1990.

Booher, Dianna. *Good Grief! Good Grammar*. New York: Fawcett Crest, 1988.

Diamond, Harriet and Phyllis Dutwin. *Grammar in Plain English*. New York: Barrons Educational Series, Inc., 1989.

Freeman, Morton S. *The Wordwatcher's Guide to Good Writing and Grammar*. Cincinnati, Oh.: Writer's Digest Books, 1990.

Gordon, Karen Elizabeth. *The Transitive Vampire, A Handbook of Grammar for the Innocent, the Eager, and the Doomed*. New York: Times Books (Random House), 1984.

————. *The Well-Tempered Sentence, A Punctuation Handbook for the Innocent, the Eager, and the Doomed*. New York: Ticknor and Fields, 1983.

Hodges, John C., et al. *Harbrace College Handbook of Grammar*. San Diego, Calif.: Harcourt, Brace, Jovanovich, 1990.

Manhard, Stephen J. *The Goof-Proofer*. New York: Collier Macmillan, 1987.

Phi Delta Kappa. *Write Right*. Bloomington, In.: Phi Delta Kappa, 1988. (Phi Delta Kappa, Box 789, Bloomington, Indiana 47402.)

Pinckert, Robert C. *Pinckert's Practical Grammar*. Cincinnati, Oh.: Writer's Digest Books, 1986.

Princeton Language Institute, ed. *21st Century Grammar Handbook*. New York: Bantam/Doubleday Dell, 1993.

Shertzer, Margaret D. *The Elements of Grammar*. New York: Collier Macmillan, 1986.

# INDEX

## A

A–Z Method 33, 34–38
  Code 35
  Dry run 36
  Paperdex™ 34–35
  Speed filing 88–9
  Tab positions 36
Acceptances 124
Account
  Checking 150
  Savings 141
Accountant 137, 146
Accounts payable 137, 142, 166
Accounts receivable 137, 141, 149, 166
Action Box 12
Action Notebook 68–69, 74, 170
Action papers
  Managing 63–70
  Task specific 66, 68
  Time specific 66
Active files 90
Activities, managing 71–6
Ad copy 108
Addresses 73, 76
Advances 154
*ADMINISTRATIVE AREA* 19, 180

ADMINISTRATIVE category 101–05
*Adventures of Huckleberry Finn* 89
Agents 118
*Alice in Wonderland* 223
Alphanumeric code 33
Annual reports 154
Answering machine 198–99
Antivirus program 185
Appointment book 163
APT 227
Area codes 77
Areas, examples of
  *ADMINISTRATIVE AREA* 19, 180
  *FINANCIAL AREA* 19, 139, 180
  *MANUSCRIPTS AREA* 19, 180
  *MARKETING AREA* 19, 117, 180
  *REFERENCE AREA* 19, 180
Areas/Categories List 18–19, 21, 82, 180
Art notes 106, 124
Articles 154
*As You Like It* 207
Association for Psychological Type 227
Associations 77
Attending preferences 211
Audits 165

Automated Teller Machine 153
Automatic backup feature 183
Automatic bank withdrawal 152

**B**

Backburner Pending Papers 64,
  69–70, 170
Backing up computer files 92, 179,
  183–84
Bank deposit slips 144, 147, 150–51,
  153
Bank statements 141, 144, 151–153,
  163
Bank transfers 154
Bank withdrawals 152
Basic Principles of Organization 206
Beethoven, Ludwig van xiii
Bellow, Saul 79
Bibliographies 106
Bill of Rights 29
Bills 144–45, 151
Birthday/Holiday List 77
Books 58, 77, 103, 203
Bookshelves 191, 204
Borrowing 77
Boxes, filing and storage 201
Braine, John 187
Brainstorming technique 93
*Brave New World* 167
Briggs, Katharine C. 210
Brochures 122
Budget 138
Bulky envelopes 59
*The Burden of Proof* 135
Business contacts 77
**BUSINESS AND LEGAL
  REFERENCE** 19
Buyers, targeting 117

**C**

Calendars 72, 163
Calls   See Telephone
Canceled checks   See Checks
CAPT 227
Car expenses 144
Cash Disbursements 137, 139
Cash Disbursements Code List
  156–57, 159–60
Cash Disbursements Ledger 156,
  159–60, 166
Cash Disbursements Summary
  160–62, 166
Cash Disbursements Update Form
  143
Cash inflow 147
Cash outflow 151
Cash Receipts Code List 140,
  153–54, 156
Cash Receipts Ledger 153, 155–56,
  166
Cash Receipts Summary 160–61, 166
Cash Receipts Update Form 140, 166
Cash receipts/receivables 137, 139
**CATALOGS** category 42
Categories
  Codes for 21, 39
  Naming 21
Categories, examples of
  **ADMINISTRATIVE** 101–05
  **BUSINESS AND LEGAL
    REFERENCE** 19
  **CATALOGS** 42
  **COMPUTER PURCHASE** 170
  **CREDITS AND CLIPS** 21, 28,
    121, 128–29, 180
  **CRIMINALS IN HISTORY** 53
  **DROPPED PROJECTS** 102, 113
  **EDITING CLIENTS** 42

**238**

EXPENSES 19, 39, 85, 139, 142–44, 160, 162, 164, 166
FINANCIAL 164
FORMS 19
GENERAL REFERENCE 19, 34–5
GEOGRAPHY 57
GREAT BRITAIN 55
GROUPS/ORGANIZATIONS 21, 38
HEALTH AND NUTRITION 44
IDEAS 19, 21, 28, 39, 44, 85, 97–101, 180
IN LEFT FIELD 39
INCOME 19, 85, 139, 140–41, 144, 148–49, 154, 156, 161, 163–64, 166
INSECTS 53
LOON BOOK PROJECT 107–08, 180
MARKETING ACTION 19, 119–28
MARKETING LEADS 19, 21, 28, 39, 117–19, 180
MARKETING REFERENCE 117–19
MASTERS 19
MOLLY ON THE OVERLAND TRAIL 19, 28
MONTHLY TRANSACTIONS 19, 139, 144–145, 151–52, 163–64
MYSTERY 54
ONGOING PROJECTS 108
PAST PROJECTS 19, 124
POETRY 58
PROJECTS 19, 101, 103
RESEARCH 106–08
REVOLUTIONARY WAR 56
SAN FRANCISCO HISTORY 36
SCIENCE 57
SCREENWRITING GUILD 39

SPORTS IN ACTION 10
TAXES 19, 139, 145–47, 162–65
WRITING 106
WRITING BUSINESS 19, 41, 92, 133, 180
WRITING GENRE 19, 39, 43
WRITING MECHANICS 19, 43, 85
WRITING SKILLS 19, 39, 43
Categorize: group subjects 18
Category Code List 82–83
CD ROM 169–71, 173
Center for Applications of Psychological Type 227
Central Processing Unit (CPU) 173
Centralize: gather papers 24
Chairs 191, 195, 197
Chapters, naming 106
Characteristics Frequently Associated With Each Type 214–15
"The Charge of the Light Brigade" 7
Charts 77
Check stubs/register 153
Checkbook 141, 150–53, 159, 180
Checking account 150
Checks 140–42, 148, 150, 152–53, 160, 163
Chinese proverb 60
Classes, materials for 14, 203
Clients lists 77
Clip Box 12–13
Clipboards 76, 109
Clipping publications 13
Clips    See Credits
Closing up at year's end 93
Clustering 20
Clutterers 3
Code-a-Pile Approach 87–8
Coded Inventory List 21–5

Codes for categories
  A–Z Method 21, 35, 39
  Prefix Method 39
Color Chart 44–5, 82–3
Color-coding 44
Columns 108, 122, 154
Commercial planners 72
Communication Log 122, 124,
  126–27
Compact disks 170
Computer 173, 206
Computer File Plan 181
Computer files/directories
  Backing up 92, 179, 183–84
  Deleting 179, 182–83
  Maintaining 182–84
  Master Index 85
  Moving 183
  Naming 177
  Organizing 177–84
  Protecting 183–84
  Storing 182–84
Computer Management Plan 177–84
Computer Priorities List 181
**COMPUTER PURCHASE** category
  170
Computer systems
  Buying 170–76
  Consumer tips 173
  Hardware decisions 172–76
  How to use 176
  Software decisions 170–72
  Upgrading 170–76
  Where to store 196
Computer terminology 171
Computer tree 180
Computerized accounting 153
Confirmation letters 78
Consolidating papers 11–13
Consulting 154

Consulting Psychologists Press 227
Conferences
  Contacts 118
  Literature 14
Containers 200–02
Contest entries 122
Contracts 77, 101, 163
Cooperative 146
Copiers 198–99, 206
Copyedited manuscripts 114, 124
Corporation, definition 146
Correspondence 18, 124, 163
Cover letter 121, 124
CPP 227
Crates 201
Credenza 191, 205
Credit rating 138
Credits
  Detailed list of 128, 130–131
  Definition 128
  Summary of 128–130
  Tracking 128
**CREDITS AND CLIPS** category 21,
  28, 121, 128–129, 180
**CRIMINALS IN HISTORY** category
  53
Critique Group 73
Cross-referencing, 47–60
  From one category to another 57
  Information from books 58
  Interfiling 52, 54
  Items too large for folder 59
  Reasons for 50
  REMINDER 58–9
  SEE 50–5
  SEE ALSO 55–6
  When to cross-reference 60
Cubicle   See Office
Curriculum materials 14, 103, 122,
  154

**D**

Daily To Do List   See To Do Lists
Databases 170
Deciding preferences 211
Deciding which filing method 43
Declaration of Independence 195
Deductions 164
Deleting computer files 179, 182–83
Deposit slips   See Bank deposit
    slips
Desk 191, 195
Desk return 195
Desktop 69–70
Desktop organizer   See Organizers
Detailed Credits List 128, 130–31
Dialogue 73, 100
Diamond, I.A.L. 61
Dickens, Charles 115
Dig-In-and-Do-It-Day 9
Direct-mail orders 140
Directions to places 76–77
Directories
    Creating 179–80
    Deleting 179, 182–83
    Organizing 181–82
    Planning 179
    Storage 183
Disaster Recovery Plan 85, 90–3
Disasters, on computer 90–91,
    184–85
Discarding papers 11, 18, 89–90,
    112
Disk back ups 92, 179, 183–84
Disk drives 172
Disks 170, 171, 176, 179, 181, 183
Documents/Action(s)/Deadline
    exercise 5, 63
Dome® bookkeeping system 155,
    159

Drafts 89–90, 101, 106, 112, 114
Drawers In and Near Desk/Away
    from Desk exercise 69, 202
Dropped projects   See Projects

**E**

Editing 154
EDITING CLIENTS category, 42
Eight Key Paper Questions, 14–15
Electric outlets, 192
Electromagnetic Interference (EMI)
    185
Electronic organizers 77
Emergency procedures 91
Energizing preferences 211
Equipment, space for 195–99
Ergonomics 196
Evaluating papers' worth 14–15
**EXPENSES** category 19, 39, 85, 139,
    142–44, 164, 166
Expenses, tracking 153–62
Extraversion, extravert preference
    211–12, 217

**F**

A *Farewell to Arms* 112
FAX machine 198–99
    Card 172
    Expenses 144
    Transmissions report 77, 144
Feature articles 101
Feeling preference 211, 213, 217
Fiction 99
File Box 12, 15
File folders
    Color options 45
    Hanging 28

File folders (*cont.*)
Interior 45
Labeling 37, 42
Manila 28
Third-cut manila 28
File Locations Sketch 83–4, 202
File managers 170, 179
Filing cabinets 191, 200–01, 205
Filing, getting help 217
Filters, monitor 196
**FINANCIAL AREA** 19, 139, 180
Financial categories
**EXPENSES** category 19, 39, 85, 139, 142–44
**FINANCIAL** category, 64
**INCOME** category 85, 139, 144, 148–49, 154, 156, 161, 163–64, 166
**MONTHLY TRANSACTIONS** category 139, 144–45, 151–52, 163–64
**TAXES** category 145–47, 164, 180
Financial records
Cash Disbursements Summary 160–62, 166
Cash Receipts Summary 160–61, 166
How long to keep 166
Why keep 137
Fitzgerald, F. Scott 13, 229
Five-Step Organization Plan 10–28, 232
Five-Step Computer Management Plan 177–82
Four-Step Maintenance Plan 81–9
Floppy disks 171, 176, 179, 181–83
Floppy drives 173
Fluorescent lights 192
Folders   See File Folders
Food editor 51
**FORMS** category 19

Forms
Cash Disbursements Update Form 143
Cash Receipts Update Form 140, 166
Communication Log 122, 124, 126–127
Computerized 184
Daily To Do List 75
Invoice 147–49
Marketing Overview Form 122, 127–28
Marketing Record Form 122, 124–26, 132–33
Ongoing Projects Log 109, 111–12, 123
Potential Markets Form 118, 120, 124–25, 132–33
Projects Overview Form 109–10
Project Status Form 109–11
Four-Step Maintenance Plan 81–9, 93
Franchise 146
*From Here to Eternity* 95
Frost, Robert 47
Front Burner Pending Papers 64–9
Future projects   See Projects

**G**

Galley/blue line 124
**GENERAL REFERENCE** category 19, 34–5
Generalize: identify your papers 15
**GEOGRAPHY** reference category 56
George, Jean 1
Ghostwriting 122, 254
Goals 71, 73, 74
*Gone with the Wind* 97

Goodman, Ellen 65
Grants 154
**GREAT BRITAIN** category 55
*Great Expectations* 115
Grouping subjects 18
**GROUPS/ORGANIZATIONS**
category 21, 38

**H**

Haley, Alex 133
Hanging folders   See File folders
Hard copy 171, 179, 181
Hard drive 171, 173, 176
Hardware 171, 172
**HEALTH AND NUTRITION**
category 44
Hemingway, Ernest 112
Hirsh, Sandra 210
Holidays 77
Home office deductions 164
*The Horn Book Magazine* 100
How-to instructions 77
Human Interest 99
Huxley, Aldous 167

**I**

IBM 170, 179, 185
Ideas 73, 97, 108
**IDEAS** category 19, 21, 26, 28, 39,
44, 85, 97–101, 180
Identifying papers to organize 15
**IN LEFT FIELD** category 39
In the Bin for Din 90
Inactive records 4, 12, 70, 90, 113,
124–25, 145, 166
Incoming cash 147

**INCOME** category 19, 85, 139,
140–41, 144, 148–49, 154, 156,
161, 163–64, 166
Income, tracking of 153–62
Incoming product orders 140
Independent contractors 164
Index cards 98
Inflow transactions 147
**INSECTS** category 53
Interest statements 163
Interface card 173
Interfiling 52, 54, 87
Interim File 85–87
Interior file folders   See File
folders
Interview notes 101, 106
Introversion, introvert preference
211–12, 217
Intuition, intuitive preference,
211–12, 217
Intuitive/judging organizational style
222–23
Intuitive/perceptive organizational
style 224–25
Inventory List 15–18, 20–1
Coding of 21–3
Creating 16–17
Sorting of 25–6
Inventory, product 138, 163
Invoices 92, 141, 144, 147–49, 151,
163
IRS 138, 152, 164–66
Issues 100

**J**

Jefferson, Thomas 195
Joint venture 146
Jones, James 95

Judging preference 211, 213, 217
Jung, Carl 210

# K

Key questions for evaluating paper
    14–15
Keyboard 173–74, 196–97
Kummerow, Jean 210

# L

L'Engle, Madeleine 132
Labeling file folders 37, 42
Laptop computer 174, 176
Ledgers
    See Cash Disbursements
    See Cash Receipts
    See Summarizing, financial
Lending/borrowing 77
Letter trays 65, 78
Letter-head 77
Letters, model 78
Library of Congress Manuscript
    Division 29
*LifeTypes* 210
*A Light in the Attic* 31
Lighting 193
Limited partnership 146
Living preferences 211
Loans 142, 154
Location (where I put what) 77
Longfellow, Henry W. 58
**LOON BOOK PROJECT** category
    107–08, 180
Loose papers 11

# M

Mac 170, 179, 185
Magazines 13, 77–8, 119
Maintenance, computer files 182
Maintenance, four-step plan 81–9,
    93
Manila folders    See File folders
Manuals 58, 77, 103, 203
Manuscripts
    Copyedited 114, 124
    Drafts 89–90, 106, 114
    Final versions 114, 124
    Submitting 120–21
    Targeting buyers for 54–5
    Weeding 89–90
    Where to file
        Current 101–08
        Dropped 102, 113, 124
        Inactive 113–14
        Past 124
*MANUSCRIPTS AREA* 19, 180
Maps 77, 101, 106
Marketing
    Follow-up 78, 132–33
    Letters 108
    Past 124
    Tips 118–19
    Tracking 122–28
    Trends 118
**MARKETING ACTION** category 19,
    119–28
*MARKETING AREA* 19, 117, 180
**MARKETING LEADS** category 19,
    21, 28, 39, 117, 180
Marketing Overview Form 122,
    127–28
Marketing Record Form 122,
    124–26, 132–33
**MARKETING REFERENCE**
    category 117–19

Marking items to file 37, 42
Master Index 81–5, 87
Master To Do List    See To Do Lists
**MASTERS** category 19
MBTI® 209–11, 226
Memo rack 65
Memory, computer 172–73
Memos 77
Mileage Log Book 144, 163
Minimize: discard & consolidate
    paper 11–15
Miscellaneous 18, 154
Mitchell, Margaret 97
Model Correspondence Notebook
    78, 121, 184
Modem 172, 175
**MOLLY ON THE OVERLAND
    TRAIL** category 19, 28
Momentum 88
Monitor 172–74
Monitor, filter 196
**MONTHLY TRANSACTIONS**
    category 139, 144–45, 151–52,
    163–64
Motivation to file 4, 218, 220, 222,
    224, 231–32
Mouse 172–74
*My Side of the Mountain* 1
Myers, Isabel Briggs 210
Myers-Briggs Type Indicator® 209
**MYSTERY** category 54

**N**

Naming categories 21
Naming computer files 177
Networking 172, 175
Newsletters 78, 108, 119, 122
Newspapers 13
Noncurrent work 71

Nonfiction 99
Nonpending papers    See Papers
Notebook computer 174
Novels 154

**O**

Obscure items 54
Off-site storage 71, 92, 184, 204
Office
    Designing 190, 204
    Equipment 195–99
    Layout 190–94
    Remodeling 190
    Space for storage 202–04
    Space to file 199–202
    Space to work 194–98
    Supplies 70, 203
Often-Out, Seldom-Stashed 70, 77
On-the-road recordkeeping 163
One-Minute Mess Test 4, 45
**ONGOING PROJECTS** category
    108
Ongoing Projects Log 109, 111–12,
    123
Order forms 77
Order, restoring 113
Orders, incoming 140
Organization, principles of 204
Organizational style 28, 216
Organizational Style Charts 218–25
Organizations/associations 77
Organize: file papers 27
Organizers 66–67
    Desktop 64–7, 74, 77, 170
    Electronic 77
Outgoing cash 151
Outlets 192, 196
Outlines 101, 106, 111
Overdrafts 138

**P**

Paid bills 151
Pamphlets 78
Paperdex™ 27, 33, 34, 37, 38, 41, 84
Paperflow For Shorter and Longer
    Projects 102
Papers
    Action 63, 66, 68
    Backburner Pending 64, 69–70
    Front Burner Pending 64, 65–9
    Nonmanuscript 101
    Nonpending 4–5, 69–71, 90, 114,
        202
    Pending 4–5, 90, 202, 206
    Presorting 85
    Protecting 85, 90–3, 183–4
Partnership, definition 145
Passbook 141
Past Marketing Action 124
**PAST PROJECTS** category 113–14,
    124
Past projects   See Projects
Patronius, Calius 9
Payroll books 163
Pencil, why 44
Pending papers   See Papers
People profiles 101
Perceptive preference 211, 213,
    217
Periodicals   See Magazines
Permanent records 92
Permissions 106
Persevering 28, 129
Personality type 28, 209–10, 226–27
    Determining 210
    Factoring in other influences 226
    Learning more about 226–27
Phone   See Telephone
Photocopied articles 78, 106
Photos 101, 106

Picchione, Nicolas 155, 159
Plan of Attack, 28
Planning Notebook 69, 71–74, 109,
    181
Planning notes, 101, 106
Plutarch 232
**POETRY** category 58
Portable 69, 201
Post-it™ Note Approach 24–5
Postal center 203
Postcards 77
Posting
    Expenses 156–60
    Income 153–56
Potential Markets Form 118, 120,
    124–25, 132–33
Prefix Method 33, 38–42
    Code 18, 39–40
    Dry run 41
    Paperdex™ 38–9
    Speed filing 88–9
    Tab positions 40–1
    Variation 42
Prefix-Alphabetic Method 42
Premarket plans 118, 120, 133
Presentation materials 203
Presorting 85
Press releases 108
Principles of organization 204
Printer 172–74, 196
Priorities List 28, 181
Prioritize 28
Product inventory 138, 163
Product orders 140
Profile of an NJ 223
Profile of an NP 225
Profile of an SJ 219
Profile of an SP 221
Profit/loss 137
Project mechanics 105
Project Status Form 109–11

Projects
  Categories 101–08
  Dropped 102, 113, 124
  Flow of 102
  Handling multiple 109
  Longer 103–08
  Ongoing 108
  Past 102, 113–14, 124
  Schedule 74–5, 105
  Shorter 101–03
  Tracking 109–12
Projects Overview Form 109–10
Proof of payment 152
Proposals 78, 120, 122, 124–25
Protecting vital documents 85, 90–3,
  183–4
Protectors, surge 185
Pruning files   See Discarding
Publicity 108
Publishers' catalogs 119
Publishing houses, keeping track of
  118
Purging papers   See Discarding

**Q**

Queries 78, 120, 122, 124–25
Questions Box 12–13, 26
Question mark code 22
Quick-Grab Organizer 77
Quick-Read Tray 77–8
Quick-Reference Notebook 77, 176

**R**

Radio Frequency Interference (RFI)
  185
Receipts 142, 144, 151–52, 163
Reconciling 151–52
Record Retention Schedule 85, 90

Recycling 12
*REFERENCE AREA* 19, 180
Reference books 203
Refiling 12
Reimbursements 150, 152
Rejection slips 124, 132–33, 163
REMINDER cross-references 50,
  58–60
Repetitive stress injury 197
Requests for changes 124
**RESEARCH** category 101, 103–04,
  106–08
Research papers 101, 106–08
Research sources 108
Responsibilities, tracking 71, 105
Restoring order 113
Resumés 121, 129, 154
Retention 85, 90, 166
Retrieval time statistics 34
**REVOLUTIONARY WAR**
  **REFERENCE** category 56
Risk management 92
Rolodex® 76–7
"The Road Not Taken" 47
Room arrangement styles 204
*Room at the Top* 187
*Roots* 133
Rotating caddy 70
Rough drafts   See Drafts
Routine information 76
Royalty check 150, 154

**S**

Safe deposit box 92
Sales tax 146–47, 151, 154
**SAN FRANCISCO HISTORY**
  category 36
SASE 121, 133
Savings account 141

Scanlon, Susan 226
Scanner 169, 172–73, 175
Schedule, writing 105
Schedules 71, 77
**SCIENCE** reference category 57
**SCREENWRITING GUILD** category
   39
Secret to paper control 4–5, 63
SEE cross-reference 34, 38, 50–5
*Seize the Day* 79
SEE ALSO cross-reference 55–6
Self-addressed, stamped envelope
   121, 133
Sensing/judging organizational style
   218–19
Sensing/perceptive organizational
   style 220–21
Sensing preference 211, 212, 217
Shakespeare, William 207
Shipping/handling 154
*Shoe* cartoon 49, 57
Short story 101
Silverstein, Shel 31
*Simplified Monthly Bookkeeping*
   *Record* 155, 159
Sketch of
   File location 82–4, 202
   Office layout 191
   Workspace 16
Sketches 101, 106
Slides 203
Software 171
Sole proprietorship, definition 145
*Some Like It Hot* 61
SORT code 22
Sorting an Inventory List 25–6
Space
   For equipment 195–99
   To File 199–202
   To Store 202–04
   To Work 194–99

Speaking 154
Speed-File Approach 88–9
Spiraling 232
**SPORTS IN ACTION** category 108
Spreadsheets 170
Staggered approach for tabs 36, 40
Statute of limitations 166
Step rack 65
Storage
   Boxes 90
   Off-site 71, 92, 184, 204
   Space 191
   Units 204
Storing personal items 203
Straight-line approach for tabs 41,
   86, 106
Subject headings 51, 88
Submitting manuscripts 119–21,
   123, 127
Summarizing, financial
   Cash Disbursements Summary
      160–62, 166
   Cash Receipts Summary 160–61,
      166
Supplies
   Office 70, 203
   Personal 203
Surge protector 185

**T**

Tab Positions
   A–Z Method 36
   Prefix Method 40–1
Tables 191
Tape backups 97, 179, 183–84
Task specific action papers 66, 68
Tax-related papers
   Audits 165
   Deductions 164

**248**

Tax-related papers (*cont.*)
Loss 164
How long to keep 166
Questions to ask 162
1040 form 166
1099 form 162
W-2 form 162
What to keep 163
Where to keep 164
Reference information 146
Returns 146, 163
Sales tax 146–47, 151, 154
**TAXES** category 145–47, 164
Telephone
Expenses 144
Location of 70
Messages 72, 101
Numbers 73
Tennyson, Alfred, Lord 7
Thank you letters 78
Themes 100
Thinking preference 211, 213, 217
Third-cut folders   See File folders
*This Side of Paradise* 229
Tickler File 67–8, 74
Time management 71
Time specific action papers 66
To Be Deposited 140, 148–50, 154, 163
To be papers
To be called 66, 68
To be filed 66, 85
To be given to 66, 68
To be done 68
To Do lists 68–9, 71, 73–5, 181
Daily To Do 75
Master To Do 69, 71, 73, 75, 181
Toss box 12
TOSS code 23
Tossing papers   See Discarding
Totes 201

Trade magazines 119
Transactions 141, 144, 148
Transfer code 23
Transfering papers 13, 23, 90, 144
Transparencies 203
Tracking
Credits and clips 128
Income 153–62
Expenses 153–62
Marketing 122–28
Writing projects 109–12
Responsibilities 71, 105
Trends 118, 122
Travel 77, 163
Turow, Scott 135
Twain, Mark 89–90
24-Hour Turn-Around Rule 133
Type   See Personality type
The Type Reporter 226
Typewriter 198

**U**

Uninterrupted Power Supply (UPS) 185
Unpaid bills 137

**V**

Vertical sorter 65
Vicinity 87
Virtual reality 169
Viruses 185
Visuals 203
Vital documents 90–3

**W**

W-2 Form 162
Wage/withholding reports 163

Wastebasket 13, 114
Weeding unneeded papers   See
    Discarding
Wilder, Billy 61
Wiring 192, 196
Withdrawals from bank 152
Wood, Don and Audrey 98
Word processing program 170–71
Word processors 198
Work associates 77
Work style 204
Workspace   See Office
Workspace inventory 85
"The Wreck of the Hesperus" 58
A Wrinkle in Time 132
Writer's Market 119, 121, 126
The Writer 164
Writers' conferences   See
    Conferences
Writers' Digest 164

Writer's Tool Kit 74, 109, 184
**WRITING** category 106
**WRITING BUSINESS** category 41,
    92, 133, 180
**WRITING GENRE** category 19, 39,
    43
**WRITING MECHANICS** category
    19, 43, 85
**WRITING SKILLS** category 19, 21,
    39, 43

**Y**

Year-End Checklist 93
Yellow pages/services 77

**Z**

Ziggy 66

# File...Don't Pile!®
# Writer's Tool Kit

The Writer's Tool Kit includes 15 camera-ready masters for forms writers use most often - such as Telephone/Fax Log, Project Status Form, Marketing Records Form, and others described in File...Don't Pile!® For People Who Write. Time-tested and successful, these popular forms will help you:
- Manage your office
- Track your writing projects from start to finish
- Market your manuscripts

You'll also find tips on how to design your own forms. Printed on quality paper, these masters are long-lasting and affordable - less than $1.00 per form! Only $14.95

The books FILE...DON'T PILE!® and FILE...DON'T PILE!® FOR PEOPLE WHO WRITE are available at your local bookstore or may be ordered directly from St. Martin's Press, 175 Fifth Avenue, New York, NY 10010 or call 1-800-221-7945.

- - - - - - - - - - - - - - - - - - - - - - - - - - - - - - - - - - - - - - - - - - - -

## ORDER FORM

Name_____

Address_____

City/State/Zip_____

| Quantity | Item | Cost/Item | Amount |
|----------|------|-----------|--------|
| | File...Don't Pile® Cassette Tape | $14.95 | |
| | A-Z Paperdex™ (3 per pkg) | 5.95 | |
| | Prefix Paperdex™ Set (50 per pkg) | 4.95 | |
| | Get Your Feet Wet Filing Kit | 9.95 | |
| | **Special combination:** Get Your Feet Wet Filing Kit and Cassette Tape Set | 22.95 | |
| | Writer's Tool Kit | 14.95 | |

**SHIPPING INFORMATION**
- All orders shipped UPS
- Street Address required
- Canadian, AK & HI orders, enclose additional $5.50
- U.S. Funds only
- Credit cards not accepted
- Packages sent to separate address require separate shipping and handling charge

| | |
|---|---|
| Minnesota residents add 6.5% sales tax | |
| Shipping and handling | $4.50 |
| Total enclosed | |

Checks payable to: Willowtree Press

Send order to: Willowtree Press, Inc.
8108 33rd Place N.
Minneapolis, MN 55427

- - - - - - - - - - - - - - - - - - - - - - - - - - - - - - - - - - - - - - - - - - - -

Pat Dorff, a member of the National Speakers Association, has motivated audiences for 20 years with her practical, creative presentations. Contact: Willowtree Press, Inc. Dept. M, 8108 33rd Place N., Minneapolis, MN 55427 or call (612) 546-4963. Edith Fine and Judith Josephson have presented writing and grammar workshops for the past 10 years. Contact: F/J Associates, 752 San Dieguito Drive, Encinitas, CA 92024 or call (619) 943-0808.